They're off to school, now what?

A mother's guide to
rediscovering herself

They're off to school, now what?

A mother's guide to rediscovering herself

MARGIT CRUICE

MojoCircle Books

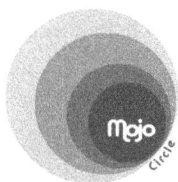

They're off to school, now what?: A mother's guide to rediscovering herself

For information about special discounts for bulk purposes, please contact:
Manager of Special Sales
MojoCircle Books
PO Box 8820
Armadale
Victoria,   3143
Australia

Cover Design: Barbeth Publications, UK
Cover Photos: PublicDomainPictures, www.pixabay.com

First paperback edition published in 2013

ISBN-13: 978-0-9580831-2-6
ISBN-10: 0958083126

At the center of your being

You have the answer:

You know who you are

And you know what you want

Lao Tzu

DEDICATION

To my mother, Gitte, who brought me up to be independent and to never give up. You continue to believe in me and support me no matter what choices I have made in life.

To my stepmother Helen, who showed me a different side to being a woman. I feel blessed that I grew up with a stepmother like you.

To my three beautiful children Rhian, Morgan and Lachlan who inspire me every day, make me laugh and help me strive to be the best person I can be. You support me through all the craziness and love me without parallel. You bring the sunshine to my life and I love you all just the way you are

CONTENTS

IN GRATITUDE

This book has been inside of me for a long time as I've been discovering myself through my own life journey. Thank you to Getrude Matshe who gave me the courage to release the author within and support me as this book came to life.

Thank you to the entire group of authors in the How to Write a Book in 40 Hours project. We created an incredible Mastermind together and each one of you is an incredible being.

Thank you to my friends and family who all believed in me, especially during those times when I didn't believe in myself. I feel blessed every day to have you all in my life.

And lastly an extra special thanks to my mother, Gitte, who helped me better explain the concepts in this book.

INTRODUCTION

This book will NOT tell you what you should do now that your children have started school. It will NOT specifically give you ideas to do things such as starting a hobby, working part-time, forming a group or any other suggestions. You see I believe that only you know what's best for you in life. I believe that by sharing some concepts I have learned over the years and asking questions, that you will find your own path. You will find what life means to you and who you want to be.

I always knew that I wanted children. I had a reasonably clear picture of how life would be – but of course, real life is nothing like that picture! I knew I wanted to stay at home while the children were young, and that as they went to school I would transition into working during school hours and be there for them after school. I would do this with a loving husband by my side, and we would make our way through life together. I would enjoy being fit and healthy, while keeping calm and composed as a mother. Instead, life took me to Spain, where I had my third child. While living halfway across the world, my husband was made redundant - and therein began an entirely new journey that did not fit in with my picture of life at all.

After returning to Australia, we thought we'd live in Brisbane, but David found it difficult to find work. He was at home with the kids and me for two years. For many people this would be a blessing, but with financial pressures beginning to loom and three young children, it felt very insecure for both of us. Thinking we were being a bit entrepreneurial, we bought a business in beautiful Noosa on the Sunshine Coast. We were excited about our new adventure and the bonus of living in one of the most beautiful places in the world.

The business had been operating for over 10 years and on the initial inspection it seemed in reasonable shape. However, once we had taken over the shop, we found the turnover was nowhere close to what we expected. Nine months later, David was diagnosed with B-Cell Lymphoma, a cancer of the blood. Our youngest child, Lachlan, was three and Morgan had just started school. Rhian was already well entrenched in school life, having started while we lived in Spain. We commenced the nightmare of hospitals, chemotherapy and seemingly endless blood transfusions.

During that time I had to help run the business, maintain the house and garden, keep up with the children's needs, cook, clean and nurse David. This wasn't matching my vision of the life I wanted at all! But we managed, and sure enough, David recovered. However, I felt an increasing sense of discontent, so not long after that, David and I decided to part. So began the journey as a single mother with three children. I had grown up with a single mother and it seemed I would follow in her footsteps, no matter that I had decided that would never be me.

We still had a business that required us to work together until we could close the shop and walk away to lick our wounds. It was a financial disaster. Everything we had worked for in the past crumbled in those few years. Now the children were all at school and the business was closed. I felt compelled to enter a time of reflection. Here I was, in my late 30s, single, three children …what the hell was I going to do? Now that I was here, I knew it was time to find a new picture. What did I really want now?

Along this journey of self-discovery, I've learned things that sound sensible, and then there are some things that I know to be true even if they sound a bit far fetched. It's in that spirit that I want to share this learning with you. Hopefully I have intertwined them with enough of my story to keep it interesting and not submerge it into a fully blown "this is how you have to do it" lecture.

Your empowerment comes from reading information that is relevant to you and then applying it in a way that makes sense in your life. The questions at the end of each chapter are designed for you to reflect on your life and make choices that feel right for you. While many of you won't bother with these, those who do will gain the clarity you desire. Enjoy the journey it leads you on, know that you deserve happiness and that you can be, do or have whatever you want out of your life.

Love and light   *Margit*

CHAPTER 1

BE HAPPY NOW

*In every moment of every day we can choose to be happy.
We become empowered when we realize that how we feel is
a choice. I do wonder why anyone would choose otherwise.*

I remember the joy and elation I felt at being a mother when I had my first child. I was excited about what this journey would bring. I had a clear vision of how it would unfold, but, of course, as almost every mother knows, that's rarely how it goes.

The concept of "being happy now" is key in our life, because at any moment, no matter what is happening around us, we can be happy. Life is about experiencing everything the world has to offer and enjoying our lives, regardless of whether we have reached our goals yet. When we can be happy now, life is easier, more fun, and we feel better about whom we are. We have the power to be happy in any moment. It is a choice that we can make any time we like.

Motherhood Myths

Society portrays several myths about motherhood that can create disharmony in our thinking about what a mother is and about our place in the world. As we become more aware of how the myths affect our feelings, we can choose to disengage from them.

Myth 1: We can do everything

We are supposed to be able to cook, clean, be the nurse, coach, tutor, mentor, wife, taxi driver and more, all with a smile on our face while exercising regularly and looking fabulous. Many are forced to work in a paid job as well. There are many incredible women in the world who appear to be able to do everything easily and well. When we observe them more closely, we discover they have found a way to think, act and create what they want in their lives because they have a clear vision of what they want.

Most women I know would love to explore life and try their hand at different activities, but few can find the time. Notice if the thought "a mother should be able to do everything" makes you feel empowered or inadequate. We don't need to listen to these myths, just be aware that they exist. We decide what works for us and what doesn't.

Myth 2: We should be perfect mothers

This myth can be torturous and leave us feeling terribly incompetent. My "perfect mother" vision included never yelling at my children, always being there when they needed me, helping them with homework and, of course being fit and healthy. My kids would feel loved, have plenty of friends, be very happy and do well at school. Instead, I do at times find myself yelling at my children and sense that they occasionally feel unloved. I remember that feeling when I was growing up, not because of anything my mother did, but because I felt insecure about myself. I had a conversation about motherhood with my mother a while ago and she made the comment "Oh, you didn't want to turn out like me," meaning that I didn't want to be a mother the same way she was. Although it sounded harsh, I realized this was true. In some ways I didn't want to be like her, but not because I thought she was bad. I just wanted to do things differently and be my version of the "perfect mother." Yet this vision is almost impossible to accomplish.

I know now that by being imperfect I offer my children a different lesson as well. I love my mother dearly and all that she brought to my life, regardless of whether or not she was perfect. I have had to learn to forgive myself for being an imperfect mother and accept that I am doing a terrific job regardless of what anyone else might think. In the end, my children love me, they know that I am there for them and that I love them … and I am finding my way in the world to be who I want to be.

Myth 3: Motherhood is totally fulfilling

I absolutely love being a mother. However, I do want an outlet to express myself that is separate from motherhood. It is such a blessing to have stay-at-home mothers who feel fulfilled because they can put so much energy into their kids. However, even when I speak to these mothers, they feel there is a social stigma because they don't want to go out and work. Whatever the choice, it's vital that all mothers feel happy with who they are and don't worry about anyone else's judgment. For those who think that motherhood should be fulfilling and then find they want more, there can also be a feeling of guilt because they're not fully satisfied. It is okay to want to express yourself in ways other than motherhood.

These 3 myths can put a lot of pressure on us to live a certain way. We all have the right to choose what's right for us. The more we can practice self acceptance and self love the more then we can start to feel an expanded sense of love, and the more comfortable we'll feel about following our chosen path. That path may change over time. When my children were young, all I wanted to do was to be at home with them and watch them grow. I wanted to make play dough, build Lego constructions and go to swimming lessons with them. Now that they are at school there are other things I want to do.

As you consider these myths and the thoughts and feelings surrounding them, you can be more conscious in the choices you make. If the myths don't make you feel good, then recognize they are myths and don't listen to them. No one other than you yourself knows what is best for you in your life.

What does it mean to be a mother in modern times?

Motherhood has certainly changed from when our mothers and grandmothers were parents, when the woman was expected to stay at home and bring up the kids. Now we have so many options and such a mix of opportunities. For some women it is a necessity to work for financial reasons. Others want to work or have a career.

The issues we face are not very different from those that our grandmothers and great grandmothers faced, but they manifest slightly differently. Like them, we face issues about confidence, time management, feeling valued and wanting our children to be healthy and happy.

Throughout the ages people have asked "who am I?" and "why am I here?" We are now in an era in which our consciousness and understanding of the greater connection that exists between us all is increasing.

What about this concept of being "just a mother?"

This is included because there are many women for whom motherhood is exactly what they want to do with their life. They find it fulfilling and have no interest in working outside the home. In the long run the only thing that's important is whether you're happy. It's doesn't matter whether others agree with your choices, but you need to be aware of the impact they have on your happiness. Some of my friends who have chosen this path feel they are undervalued and that others are judging them for their choice. We all have the possibility to feel comfortable, accepting and happy about what we choose to do.

My aim is to help you to create a peaceful state of mind regardless of whether you choose to have a career. It's simple: make choices based upon what is right for YOU. If you are a person who wants to be a stay-at-home mother, but you work because other people think you should, you will be miserable. Equally, if you become a stay-at-home mother but you really want to be out working, you will also be miserable. We all deserve to be happy! Imagine for a moment what the world would be like if we were all happier. I do not believe in such a thing as being "just a mother" - it is an extraordinary job that every mother in the world does.

Why did you become a mother?

I always knew I wanted children, but I'm not sure I knew why back when I had them. Now I know – I want the experience of sharing my life, loving unconditionally and of guiding a person to fully develop into a vital adult. I want to see how I will cope with the challenges of motherhood and to feel the connection that is almost impossible to describe to someone who doesn't have children. When I first had children, I was totally focused on motherhood. I didn't think about when or if I would want to go back to work, whether I would need to go back to work, or if there would be a part of me that would remain unfulfilled. I just knew that I wanted children.

I still remember when they were all babies, looking at them and wondering who they would grow up to be, what sort of challenges we would face and whether we would always be happy together. I am absolutely thrilled to be a mother. I feel completely blessed every day that I have my three children in my life. I know I can't control a child, but I believe I can guide and direct them and help them learn and grow. I firmly believe that it is one of the most rewarding, incredible and challenging roles we can have in this lifetime. I embrace it fully, I love it and I learn from it every day.

What if I'm feeling restless in my life?

I love to be on the go and participating in projects. When I became a mother, it felt like everything came to a halt and my entire focus and attention was on my baby. As I chose to have more children, it felt like years of being in baby-land. I enjoyed it immensely, but I started to become restless. I wanted to be a stay-at-home mother but could also feel the need to express myself in the world. As I've grown older, I've come to realize that our aim is to enjoy each stage of life and be happy. For example, I used to love to party and go out till late (hmmm … early morning) with my friends, but once the children came along I found I enjoyed other ways of being social.

Stages occur naturally with our children's changing ages. There's the baby-to-school stage, primary school, secondary school, college/university, empty nest and grandparent stage. With three children, the baby stage seemed to go on for many years. I've always been an avid learner so during this time I took short courses, read lots of books and pondered what I'd want to do next in my life. However, I realize that the more I appreciate the stage

I'm in, the more I can surrender and enjoy it. I appreciate my children more, I feel calmer about my life and the future I'm creating, and I feel content knowing that life is changing.

One wonderful piece of advice I received is "don't wish time away." The more fully engaged we are in the moment the more joy and happiness we will experience. Sometimes we trick ourselves into thinking "things will be better when …" We are responsible for the way we feel about life at any time. Our main priority at any time is to be happy…whatever stage of life we are at. If you feel restless, ask yourself what you can do to feel happy. It may mean being more present, changing your routine or defining your dreams; whatever it is, if you commit to feeling happy, life will improve.

Pursuing personal happiness

We focus much of our attention and energy on ensuring that our children are happy and cared for. This often means putting our own needs last. A lot of mothers don't even think about whether they are happy. As people and as mothers, it is essential that we strive for happiness. You may have heard the saying "if the mother in the household is happy, the household is happy!" The happier you are the more you give others around you permission to be happy too. We are one of the main role models for our children, and it's our responsibility to show them what it looks like to be happy.

Whatever you want out of life is your choice – basically it should feel good and do no harm to anyone. As we begin to identify our goals and dreams, it is most important to be happy in the process. Of course, there are frustrations, challenges and never-ending routines when we have children, but we have the capability to choose happiness at any time. We are here to have a joyful life experience, including the experience with our children. When our children are young and innocent, we can see the joy of life in them. This can change as they grow older and begin to develop their own beliefs, perspectives and thought patterns. Focusing on your happiness though, ends up being a gift for the whole family.

I feel like time is passing so quickly…

Time is an issue I deal with in detail in Chapter 9 because it's often the excuse mothers' use for not doing the things they would like. If you find yourself at the end of each year wondering where the year went, it may be because you have no definite goals or you feel like you are not moving forward in life. Time is nothing more than a way to measure our life. I find the more present I am to what's happening right now, the longer the time feels. When we have some small goals and acknowledge our achievements along the way we can slow down the feeling of time passing.

It's an interesting exercise to project yourself into the future and imagine yourself looking back over your life. What would you like to be able to say at the end of this year, or in 5 or 10 years? In each moment we are creating our future story – the more we know who we want to be, the more we can direct our thoughts and actions toward that vision. When our thoughts and actions are in alignment with what we want in the long term, our sense of time changes.

How can I be the best mother for my kids and rediscover myself?

I interviewed a group of women who most would consider successful. All were combining a career with motherhood. I asked their advice to mothers who are seeking to find themselves. Their answers were remarkably similar – they all basically said to make time and space for you. This didn't mean having coffee with friends; rather, they meant that it is imperative to set aside time alone for reflection to reconnect with the sense of self. We can lose ourselves in those first few years of motherhood, as the overwhelming surge of love and need to protect our children kicks in. While we are finding our way through motherhood, we find more peace by keeping sight of who we are. This means finding activities that help us feel in tune with our intuition, calm our mind and maintain a connection with Source/God/Universe/Higher self. One of the greatest gifts we can give our children and ourselves is to understand what we want out of life, to know who we are and to connect with our essence.

As you move through this process, the key is to use love as the basis for everything. Love is an extraordinary force in our world; it can transform lives. When you have great love for yourself, you take different actions, see the beauty in others and feel confident in who you are. The more you see the world through the eyes of love, the more possibilities you see and the more connected you will feel to yourself and to others. Go gently and know that you bring a unique viewpoint to the world and you are valuable, whatever your choices are.

Right here, right now

This book wouldn't be complete without some reference to the work of Ekhart Tolle's *The Power of Now*. Tolle's work is a reminder to everyone that to live most powerfully is to experience the present moment. So much of our time is spent worrying about the future, creating imaginary scenarios of what might happen or thinking about what we haven't done well enough in the past, that we miss out on what's happening in the present moment. As John Lennon so aptly said: "Life is what happens to you while you're busy making other plans". Each moment of motherhood is special, even the difficult ones! The more you can appreciate what is happening in the moment the happier you will be.

You absolutely need to set aside time to define your vision for the future and to set goals. The trick is to feel good while you are setting these goals and not to worry that you haven't reached them yet. Every thought and feeling you have now, creates your experience of the present moment as well as affecting your future. In other words, the happier you can be right now, the more happy moments you are creating in your future.

Being fully present allows us to experience everything life has to offer. When you reflect on your life, consider what your favorite memories are. It is likely that many will be of times when you felt strong positive emotions such as exhilaration, inspiration and joy. These are the moments when you share laughter with friends, feel the thrill of winning a competition, hit a home run, or the moment your child was born. At these times we are fully in the moment and our mind and heart are focused on whatever we are doing.

The little things in life

Every moment has something good to offer. The little things in life give us focus in the moment and help us engage more fully in the world. Remember the thrill of your baby's first smile…or when they learned to wave, spoke their first word, took their first steps. These occasions trigger feelings of happiness and joy. The more little things you notice, the more present you become in your life, the more you experience and the slower time passes. Those little things make you smile!

Nature is a wonderful place to notice little things. As humans we feel more grounded when we spend time in nature. Those of you who go camping or hiking will understand what I mean. Nature has a way of reenergizing us and helping us to feel calm. Nature also is full of metaphors for us to learn from … butterflies pushing their way out of a cocoon, turtles burying their eggs on the beach and knowing exactly where they are, puppies always being happy to see us. It's these little things that make nature so special, the same way little things in our life do.

The true impact of our feelings

The more I learn, the more I see how we create our experiences in life. The movie *The Secret* shows how we can manifest anything by deciding what we want and believing we can have it. The only reason we want anything in life is because of the feelings we believe it will give us. It doesn't matter if it is a new car, a different job or solving world hunger – the end result is that we will feel good. Our thoughts help to create our reality because they affect the way we feel. Our thoughts and emotions send out vibrations out into the universe, and these vibrations are mirrored back to us. The universe gives us experiences that match our feelings.

We affect the world around us – this has been demonstrated scientifically. One experiment that helped me understand this was performed in the 1990s by Vladimir Paponin. In the first part of the experiment, he created a vacuum inside a glass tube. He then measured the light photons in the tube and found them to be randomly distributed. In the second part, he took a sample of human DNA, placed it in the tube and again created a vacuum. He then measured the distribution of light photons and found *they lined up in an orderly, non-random fashion.* In the third part, he removed the DNA sample, recreated the vacuum and measured the distribution of light photons again. Expecting to see them return to their random distribution, he was surprised to find they were still lined up the way they had been when the DNA was in the tube. These results suggest that our DNA affects the world around us, but more importantly, this affect remains after we have left.

As you begin to put this information together, you will start to see just how you create your own life. Hopefully this will open up possibilities that you had not considered for yourself. Our feelings impact:

- the way we experience life in the present moment
- our experiences of others through the mirroring affect
- our future through the vibrations we emit
- our DNA, which in turn, has a physical effect on the world

Our emotional state is of great importance in our life, yet we often believe we are victim to our emotions. There are many ways we can improve our state of feeling. I sincerely hope that, in this book, you will find some ideas that will appeal to you and that you will summon the courage to put some of them into action.

What does true happiness feel like?

Have you ever stopped to think about what happiness feels like for you? While we can identify the feeling, it is harder to describe. When we are happy, we generally don't think about how we look or whether we are good enough – we are consumed by the present moment. True happiness exists in your heart space. It doesn't require anything outside of us. Often we believe that we will be happy when our partner changes, when we have more money, when we know our purpose in life, when we lose weight or any number of other things. We can choose to feel happy at any time we want, without anything changing in our life.

A while ago, I took my son to Australia Zoo. I watched his face as he ran from animal to animal. He was totally in the moment and experiencing the pure joy of being there. Everything fascinated him, from the bird show to the elephants. He was chattering away and asking questions. Lachlan brought a smile to the face of many others that day as he expressed his joy of exploring the zoo. Young children are beautiful examples of living from a place of happiness. Theirs is a natural expression of what exists in their hearts, and they are not afraid to show it to the world.

Chapter Summary

Being happy is a choice we can make in any moment, although it may not always be easy. However, we are also supposed to experience a range of emotions; being happy now is not meant to block that experience, rather encourage us to move out of negative emotions faster. If our focus is on happiness or on being happier than we currently are, we will raise our vibration and attract more events that bring happiness.

Motherhood myths can leave us feeling less than happy about our mothering efforts and who we are as people. Once we recognize that these are mere myths, we can evaluate how much of our feeling is based upon society ideals that no one can live up to. Most mothers, working or not, feel similar stresses such as the struggle to be an individual, ensuring their children are well looked after and losing confidence in their abilities after being at home. If we can focus on our happiness and that of our family we may find decision-making becomes simplified. The best gift we can give ourselves and our family is to be fully present with them. To experience the present moment and enjoy what life has to offer is a surefire path to happiness. Our emotions impact on what we create in our future and our immediate sense of wellbeing. We saw that our DNA affects the world around us and that this affect lasts after we have left. Our emotional state is the most important thing we can work on to create change in our life.

Questions for self-reflection

1. How am I feeling most of the time?

_____

_____

_____

_____

_____

2. What would it mean to me to be totally happy?

_____

_____

_____

_____

_____

3. What is one thing I can start changing to feel happier?

_____

_____

_____

_____

_____

CHAPTER 2

YOU ARE WHAT YOU THINK

Who we are is a reflection of what we think at our deepest level. If we think we are love and light we will walk with that energy. If we think we are damaged and need healing that will also show.

Some of the concepts I discuss in this chapter may feel uncomfortable to some readers. If it doesn't resonate with you, try keeping an open mind and see what happens. Imagine that we are pure energy and that our brain and heart send signals out into the world, like a radio transmitter. This would mean our every thought gives out energy. Every thought we have tells the universe what we think about life, about ourselves and about others. The universe then brings experiences and situations that perfectly reflect your thinking. This is the Law of Attraction concept shared in the movie *The Secret.*

Every single thought we have has power. Every time you think, "I can't do it," that message is sent out to the universe. In such cases you create situations that make you feel overwhelmed, inadequate, and that you are unable to do anything well. We need to be aware what we are thinking every moment of every day, of how we are limiting ourselves and how we see our lives. My life with my three children is challenging, fun and lively. They reflect back to me everything that's going on inside me; they are the greatest indicators of my thinking. As we live together, we constantly pick up on each other's energy.

When I was growing up I had an image of my sister as the family's creative person and of myself as the sporty one. I let this thought limit me for years. I couldn't draw well and I still can't. However, I have realized that creativity comes in innumerable different forms. Now I really enjoy painting, especially with my children (all abstract!) We have beautiful artwork hanging around our home that we have completed together. It finally dawned on me that I had refrained from painting because I had decided that I wasn't good at it. We think these kinds of thoughts every day; we decide we can't do things then don't bother trying because we think we can't. Any thought energy we send out of "I can't do it" or "it's too hard" help to create experiences where life doesn't work out.

The impact of our thoughts

Have a look around the room or wherever you are now. Everything began with a thought. The chair you are sitting on, the table in the lounge room, the kitchen bench, the car you are driving. Every single thing in your life was created by someone at some point and came from a thought. It didn't just magically appear. The same is true with our lives. When we begin to look back on our lives, we can see how connected everything is, how one situation led to another and another. In every situation, your thinking led you along the way. When we want to create change in our lives, we must start by changing our thinking. When you change your thinking, your experiences will change.

Our thoughts really are just a starting point. Once you understand that every thought has an effect on your life, you begin to be more conscious about what you are thinking, especially if you want to create a change for the better. YOU get to decide how you think about yourself and the world. Your past, skills, knowledge or your experience does not need to limit you as long as you have some imagination. You can be anything and anyone you want to be, but it must start with you changing the way you think about yourself … the way you see yourself.

Thoughts have a physical effect on our body

Every time we think a thought, our brain releases a chemical into our body. In it's simplest form, positive thoughts release chemicals that make us feel happy, and negative thoughts release chemicals that make us feel bad. This happens constantly in our body. From a sheer physical perspective, it is important to think positively because these chemical responses affect the way we feel. William Glasser's choice theory shows that we can directly control our thoughts and actions but not our feelings or our physiology. However, we can indirectly control our feelings and physiology through our thoughts and actions.

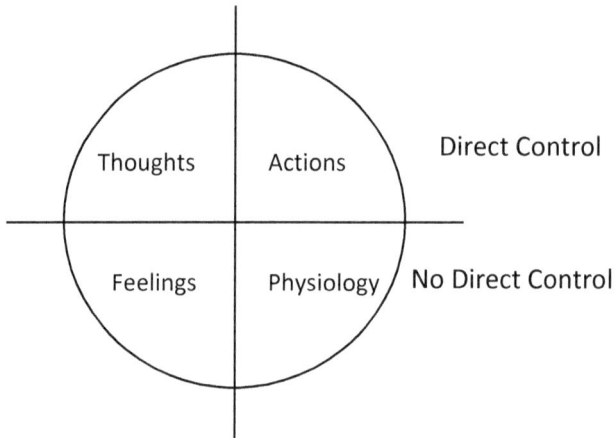

Fig 1: Glasser Choice Theory depiction of control

Most mothers I have met are very good at focusing positive thoughts on their children. It's very easy to say to a child, "You are amazing, you can do it" or "Keep going; you're doing great." But when we think in terms of ourselves, our thoughts are far from always positive. We tend to be our own harshest critic rather than our biggest supporter. Thinking happy thoughts will lead to feeling happier. Feeling happy is the key to living your life, to creating more happy situations and to identifying who you are. When we are happy, we want to be with ourselves and others want to be with us. Life becomes easier and more fun. In my journey of self-discovery, I have at times become overly serious and thought, "I have to get this right" or "I should be further ahead in my life." Thoughts like this put pressure on us and make us feel bad about where we are now. It's far more positive to think in terms of being on a journey and knowing that we are in the process of self-discovery.

Try to reflect on the negative and positive thoughts as they occur to you. If you hear yourself saying something that you don't want to be saying, then turn it around and change it. I provide some tools and techniques at the end of this chapter to help you do that. You can only change your thoughts once you become aware of what you are thinking.

How beliefs are formed

The way you think is partly determined by your beliefs, a lot of which were formed very early in your life. A belief is simply a thought that you think over and over. As we think these thoughts, we create the ensuing experience. That experience leads us to believe that our thoughts reflect "truth". We can teach ourselves to believe anything we want. For a long time I believed that if I went to work, I would lose my relationship with my kids. These thoughts, which became a belief, held me back for many years from doing the things I wanted to do because I was scared. It is essential to me to maintain my relationship with my kids. This belief became a driving force in my life, and it created a lot of conflict in me because there were things that I wanted to do. Every time I tried to move forward I wouldn't experience success.

It is important to know what our beliefs are but also to remember that many of our beliefs are stored deeply, beyond our level of awareness; it might take quite some time and effort to bring them to the surface. A careful look at what you have in your life gives you a very good indication of your beliefs. If this is the first time you attempt to go there, do go gently. We want to help open up possibilities - not feel down about where you are in your life.

Should we question everything we believe?

Absolutely! Every single belief we hold can and should be questioned. Remember, everyone has her own truth. For example, when two children have been arguing and you ask what happened, the version you will get from each child will be completely different. Both children believe their version to be true and neither of them will budge. They simply see the situation from different perspectives. We adults do the same, so we need to question our beliefs constantly to check if they are limiting or expanding. Asking questions opens up new possibilities. For example, "What work could I do that fulfills me and allows me also to be the mother I want to be?" provides numerous opportunities, whereas "I can't see how I can work and be the mother I want to be" closes us down.

For those of you who want to be a stay-at-home mother, it is essential that you feel good about it. Theoretically, motherhood is valued, but the kinds of messages we receive via the media, together with the tacit expectations of mothers in our Western society, show clearly that motherhood is grossly undervalued. Yet most mothers' highest priorities are their children. If you are feeling a little insecure and are unsure about your own role in life, try to identify the beliefs that are helping to create that uncertain situation.

As many of our beliefs were formed at a very early age, we want to make sure they are serving us as adults. My belief around being the mother I wanted to be, which conflicted with being a working mother, was created in childhood. It was not serving me as an adult but it took work to uncover it as it manifested in sneaky ways.

Why we react the way we do

Messages from the brain travel along what we call neural pathways via neurons (nerve cells) to our body and from the body back to the brain. Imagine these pathways as a tree with lots of branches emanating in the brain and communicating with other neurons in the body. Different kinds of neurons carry different types of messages that enable the body to respond in specific ways. For example, when you encounter a situation that, at some point in your life, was scary to you, your body would respond instantly: you would have experienced sweaty hands, a rapid pulse, short, shallow breaths, and a knot in your stomach. All of these combined to make you feel anxious. Every time you encounter the same, or a similar, situation, or even when you expect to encounter it, the same symptoms will appear in a flash unless you, at some other point in your life, were able to deal with the situation such that it no longer scares you. The more often you have experienced (or expected) the situation to arise, the stronger the neural pathway will become, and the harder it will be to break it. As a child, I developed an aversion towards siblings fighting; when my children argue those neural pathways automatically spring into action. The trick we must learn is to stop and think before we react and then respond consciously and constructively instead to aversive situations.

The good news is that we can change neural pathways that are not beneficial to us. This is exciting because it means we don't have to be the victim of decisions we may have made in the past. It takes 21-30 days to change a neural pathway. Therefore, there is some truth to the literature telling us to persevere with a new habit for at least 21-30 days for it to become a natural part of life.

If you recognize that you have some beliefs you need to change, know that this is possible, albeit with some effort. We can change any thought or perception about who we are and consciously choose to be whoever we want to be. Of course, big changes do not happen overnight, but if you work at it you will change because ANYONE can. Don't be discouraged if, after 10 or 14 days, you feel no change. If you persevere at developing new neural pathways, you will eventually find that the new habit has become automatic.

Am I who think I am?

We are all who we think we are in one way; in another way, we are nothing like we think we are. When I ask my friends how they see me, I get a very different perspective from my own. Our own self-perception is often quite different from that of others. We are all so much more than what we ourselves realize. We have so many more capabilities, talents and skills than we recognize in ourselves. Unfortunately modern society does not teach us to recognize these.

As we send energy out into the universe, we create our life from the perspective and beliefs we have about ourselves. In that way we become what we think. Everything that occurred in our past did so because of the way we thought. Life didn't just happen. The way we choose to look events in our life is totally up to us. The most important question to ask is, "Who do I want to be?" That is a lifelong question, because we will re-invent ourselves several times. For mothers, one of those times is when our children begin school.

How we limit ourselves

Many people are taught to think small, to stop dreaming or to get real about what is possible in their lives. Alternatively, we may think small to protect ourselves from hurt and disappointment based upon our past experiences. The more we think small, the more we limit ourselves. We can do anything we want; yet when we ask ourselves what we want, we are guided by what seems reasonable. If we open our heart and mind to bigger opportunities and to our secret dreams, the world responds to us and helps us to realize those dreams. By closing yourself to opportunities or to thinking big, you limit yourself.

We tend to assume that our patterns of thinking are normal, or we may not think about our thinking at all. As these habitual patterns develop in childhood, we need to relearn how to think. My own thinking patterns about being a working mother included many misconceptions, but once I began to change those patterns, the outcomes also changed. I developed a new, healthier belief in my dreams and myself, which opened up wonderful opportunities for my whole family.

The water experiments of Dr. Emoto

Dr. Masaru Emoto, a Japanese scientist has conducted some intriguing experiments with water. He took water samples from different places around the world and froze them. He then spliced and magnified them under a powerful microscope enabling him to see the emerging crystal structures. One finding was that water from a polluted source, like a dam in Japan, formed no structure at all but remained an unattractive, messy shape. By contrast, water from a natural spring formed stunning snowflake-like crystals. Water from different sources thus formed different crystal structures, and the beauty of the shape was influenced by the source.

In another experiment he again took water from the polluted dam in Japan and asked some Buddhist monks to pray over it. Astonishingly, the water crystals *physically changed* their formation into structures similar to the original crystals from the natural spring. In other experiments he labeled his water samples with different words such as "I love you", "I hate you", and "peace". Low, negative vibrations of words such as "hate" or "anger" resulted in unformed crystal structures. However, water labeled with positive, higher frequency words such as "I love you" or "you are peaceful" resulted in beautifully shaped crystals. Evidently, the structures changed depending on the labels. In the light of these experiments, and given that the human body is composed of 65-70% water, isn't it plausible that the words you use might affect you physically? What a good reason to be mindful about the language you use to describe yourself and others.

Dr. Emoto conducted similar experiments to determine the effect music had upon the structure of water. When playing hard rock or heavy metal music, no crystals would form, much like the water from the polluted dam. Yet, when he played classical music, the water formed beautifully shaped crystals. This suggests that we should also consider carefully the kinds of music we choose to listen to, as evidently, this also impacts our body. Sound waves create vibrations in the air, so we want to be listening to music with a high vibration rate. Evidence therefore suggests that the words we use, the thoughts we think and the music we listen to all affect how we feel. Next time you think something negative about yourself, stop and reflect for a moment on what it is doing to you.

Expand your thinking

Whatever we focus on expands. That is, whatever we choose to think about will attract more experiences. As mothers we need to be part of the mix along with our children and partners. Remember it's your thinking that creates the possibilities and you can hold yourself back by listening to all the unproductive beliefs you have formed. We must question our habitual thought patterns because they keep us in a particular desirable or undesirable cycle. We need to be clear about the things we want to bring into our lives for them to occur. This does not mean that we have to stop thinking about our families and children; rather, we expand our thinking when taking time to think about what is important to us.

"You know that two objects cannot fill the same space at the same time. Your mind can be compared to that space: you can't keep your mind filled with negative thoughts or doubts if you have it filled with positive, powerful, and creative thoughts."

Claude M Bristol,

As mothers we are often thinking about 10 different things at once, or at least we believe we are. However, only one thought can exist in your mind at a time. We like to imagine we are multi-thinking, but thoughts actually occur sequentially, one after the other, in rapid succession. To create what we want, we need to focus our attention. As we are making a transition and deciding what to do with our lives, we need to focus our attention as much as we can on what we want and feel good about. As a mother you will always have a lot to do, but you can only FOCUS on one thing at a time. Even if you try to do two or three things at a time, you are only really focused on one. For example, you can't listen fully to your child and cook dinner at the same time. Try it – you will notice that you keep shifting focus between the two.

Disciplining your mind

We can only create change through awareness. Once you notice your thinking patterns and habits, you can begin to change them. Esther and Jerry Hicks, authors of the book *Ask and it is Given,* tell us that it's *not even so much the thoughts that we are thinking that help us to create our lives, but it's how we feel about the thoughts that we think.* Even if all our thoughts are positive all the time but don't make us feel good, we will create a situation of discord that stops us from creating what we want.

How you feel tells you something about your thinking. If you are feeling unworthy, unhappy or guilty most of the time, you definitely need to change your thinking. When you question your thoughts, you can begin to see them from a new perspective. You can change the way you look at anything in your life or in the world. Sometimes it can help to pretend you are someone else looking at the situation. Anyone will do - someone famous, male, female…I prefer to choose people who inspire me and ask how he or she would see the situation. This can open up possibilities and new ways of looking at a situation.

By getting into the habit of noticing negative thoughts we can choose to shift. However, when we try to enforce positive thoughts like through affirmations, it does not always feel good. As we notice this, we need to move into a space where the thought feels good; we may need to start with a different affirmation to move toward the thought we want. Positive affirmations can have a great impact in our lives, but we need to be aware of how we feel when we are using those affirmations. Disciplining our mind means we commit to noticing and changing our thoughts to align with what we want to create.

Tools I have used to help me change my thoughts

Here are 3 tools that are very effective, yet very simple to use. I use these in my life, and I have even taught them to children at schools.

Pause button

The pause button is a standard feature of our modern world; we can pause a movie, audio or even a TV show. The same can be done with our mind. When you catch yourself thinking negative thoughts that you don't want, press the imaginary pause button. You can use this anytime you catch yourself using those lower vibrational thoughts or words. Lower vibrational words include statements like "I can't," "it's hard," or "it won't happen." Instead, replace these with something you can believe. A good question to ask yourself is, "How can I think/say this in a way that supports me?" If you are able to catch yourself in the moment, you can create a shift very quickly. Next time you are thinking about what it is you want to do with your life, take note of the thoughts that occur automatically. Do you need to hit your pause button and ask yourself if you are thinking supportive thoughts?

Wouldn't it be nice if?

This tool is best used when we need to recognize hope. As we create our lives from our thoughts and feeling, it is important to focus on thoughts that allow new possibilities to emerge rather than focusing on what is missing in our life. This helps to break down any resistance to our present situation. For example, when our children act in a challenging way, we can think, "Wouldn't it be nice if my children behaved well today?" Feel the difference from thinking "my children are so poorly behaved." It is all about shifting to a higher vibration that allows for new experiences rather than expecting instant results in a given situation.

Turn it around

Similar to the imaginary pause button, this tool takes you one step further. When you hear yourself uttering negative words, stop and think how you can turn them into something positive. While the pause button reminds you to stop for a moment, turning it around gives the challenge of turning a negative perception into something positive.

It can be a little difficult to start doing this, but with practice it will become second nature. You will change your perception of life and of the world slowly but surely. If you do find yourself stuck and unable to turn a negative into a positive thought, ask yourself "What possibility can I open up by changing my thinking around this?" That can allow something gentler to begin to break down the resistance to that thought.

Chapter Summary

Every day we think millions of thoughts, every single one of which counts. The longer we allow ourselves to stay in negative thought patterns, the further out of reach our happiness remains. Thoughts cause the brain to release chemicals into the body, which, in turn, affect us physically. Choice Theory highlights this relationship showing that we can control our thoughts and actions directly but not our feelings and physiology. However, our thoughts and actions do influence our feelings and our physiology. Thoughts therefore play a much bigger role in our life that we realize.

We all have beliefs that don't serve us. Once we understand that beliefs are simply thoughts we have had over and over again, we begin to see that we can change our beliefs. It is a matter or redirecting our neural pathways to create healthier, more supportive responses. The way we react originates in how we have stored past hurts, guilt and fears – if we have never dealt with these on an energetic level, our reactions will not always be appropriate. As our awareness of our thoughts increases, it is possible to change our automatic reactions by developing new neural pathways.

The way we perceive ourselves is not always consistent with who we are. We are harsh critics of ourselves and of our possibilities. If we could all open our hearts and minds we would see that we are all so much more than we currently believe. By sticking to those old beliefs, we continue to limit what we think is possible for us.

Masaru Emoto's water experiments showed that words have energy that can affect physical things. As we are 65-70% water, our thoughts, the words we say and music we listen to are likely to have a physical effect on us. This provides a good reason to be very aware of what we are saying and thinking in any given moment.

Engaging our imagination and dreaming about our possibilities rather than limiting ourselves to what we THINK is possible helps to expand our thinking. To do this means we have to discipline our mind and be consistent and persistent in our efforts to think and feel positive.

Tools you might like to try include:

- The Pause Button – when you think a negative thought press the imaginary pause button
- Wouldn't it be nice if – provides hope that maybe life can be different
- Turn it around – change the negative thought to a positive thought

Questions for self-reflection

1. What thoughts would I like to change?

_____

_____

_____

_____

_____

2. What would I like to change them to?

_____

_____

_____

_____

_____

3. What tool would I like to try using to change my thinking?

_____

_____

_____

_____

_____

CHAPTER 3

LOVING YOURSELF

The best gift we can give ourselves is LOVE. To recognize the value we bring to the world and show our children that this is normal could change the world within one generation.

There was a time when I found myself in a disastrous rebound relationship after my husband and I separated, when I didn't like myself very much. I was agonizing about the relationship and was in a very dark place. It felt like my world was coming to an end. In reality I was grieving the loss of my idealized picture, trying to come to terms with the fact that my life did not look like the fairy tale I had thought it would.

When I recall that time I am shocked at the person I became. I wonder how I could have had such low self-esteem, how I couldn't see the blessings in my life every day, how I allowed a situation that turned out to be perfect to interrupt the very core of who I was and disengage me from life. I wouldn't wish this experience on anyone; however, in looking back I am entirely grateful for it, for I know that I learned a valuable lesson, namely to LOVE myself.

When I was in a place of not loving myself, every day was a struggle. I couldn't move forward and I didn't have any hope. My youngest son was just starting school and I felt like I had to begin my life all over again but with three children who depended on me. Eventually, I discovered that love truly is the answer, and that through love we can do anything.

What I'm sharing in this chapter is vital for all of us to understand. It's not a scientific theory; rather it is a description of a way of life where you can find happiness beyond your wildest imagination. The more love you bring into your life, the more you will thrive. You will feel happier, more content, and you will experience the pure joy of living from such a vital life force. Love is to be celebrated and enjoyed. Loving yourself is an absolute must.

What is it about love that I need?

Love is the most powerful force in the universe. Think about it –
it's the only force that can stop a war or turn an enemy into a
friend. We can't see love, but we can feel it around us. It is one of
the highest vibrational forces known in the universe. But love is
also a verb – something that we do. It's something that we feel
inside and that resonates in our actions. Remember the very first
time you held your newborn baby and you looked at this person –
you knew instantly that you loved him/her. You knew that,
regardless of anything that might be wrong, whether they cried, or
who they would grow up to be, you would love this person for the
rest of your life. That's the sort of love I am talking about; love that
comes straight from the heart. When we get in touch with that
force we can do anything.

We can see the extraordinary in other people, and we can be
inspired and motivated by them. But when we look at ourselves, we
are far more critical. In the situation I described above when I was
at my absolute lowest in life, I remember feeling like there was
nothing that could pull me out of that abyss. I was at the opposite
end of the love spectrum. I was in fear, I felt deeply depressed, and
I couldn't see any way out of the situation I was in. I felt that life
was hopeless, that I was hopeless, and that nothing was going to
change this. As I slowly moved more into appreciation and
gratitude, I was able to shift. I now realize that if I had been able to
apply love to that situation, the entire experience would have been
very different. If I had seen the perfection in what was happening,
I would not have felt the way I did.

I share this story even though it might seem unrelated to children
heading off to school, because it was through this experience that I
realized how important it is to love myself. It was a different
struggle from deciding what to do with my life, but the lesson was
one of the most important ones in my life. Life becomes easier
when you let go of resistance and see how amazing you are. When
you love yourself fully, magic happens. The more we mothers love
ourselves, the better off our children, family, community and

society will be. Embrace love as a concept, as a feeling, and as your life force. Love your children unconditionally - and love yourself in the same way!

The reflection in the mirror

Most of us cannot compare to women we see in magazines or on TV even if we wanted … and bear in mind modern Photoshop technology! When we look in the mirror, we tend to compare ourselves to other people, and we don't see the perfection we would like to see. This can leave us feeling down, uncertain and lower our self-esteem. Next time you look in the mirror, try looking into your eyes and saying, "I love you." This is a very difficult exercise for many people that can cause an emotional response. When I first started to do this, I was very resistant. I did not want to look into my eyes and feel that unconditional love for myself – it was strange and foreign to me. If you have trouble doing this exercise persist with it, because it feels wonderful when you get there.

Our Story

When you talk about yourself, notice the words you use to describe who you are and the story of your life. At any time we can choose who we are, but every time we say something like, "Oh, that was so stupid of me," it reinforces in our mind and heart the idea that we are indeed stupid. It's much more beneficial to look at the situation and laugh. In most cases in a week or a month, most of those little situations don't matter anymore. For example, if we drop a glass and smash it, it really doesn't matter, yet in the moment we can call ourselves stupid for dropping it.

Not so long ago I used to tell people my story and about what I had been through; I found myself focusing on the negative aspects. This gave me an excuse to be where I was in life, who I was, and to have failed achieving what I wanted. Every time I repeated that story, it reinforced all those negative feelings. Instead I could have chosen to focus on how incredible it was for me to go and live in another country, to learn another language and have a baby over there, or about how I was able to stay happy while my ex-husband was out of work. Or I could mention the way I was able to manage a household, children and a business, and look after David while he was sick.

The story we tell about our lives is just a story – the story itself does not define us. Who we are and who we become through that story is far more important. When I reflect back on that time, I can honestly say I was amazing, and embrace the fact that I was successful. Listen to what you are saying about your life story and about your life. It doesn't matter if you don't know where you are going right now, but hopefully by the end of this book, you will have a clearer picture. For now, as you look back on your life, consider your successes. Move out of the negative side of your "story" of who you are and where you are and embrace yourself as a success.

The conversations we have

When I used to tell my story, other people would engage in the "poor me" side of it. They thought they were being supportive, but in reality, they were simply reinforcing my excuses. I have learned that it is normal to feel sympathy for someone and allow him or her to remain stuck. It is more supportive to hold a space for each other to move into. By that I mean allowing the possibility for people to move into the life of their dreams and to believe that they can do it. It all comes back to love!

Gossiping is another hideous infliction in our society. Gossip is anything we say about another person in their absence. Our society promotes gossip through magazines and other media including the Internet and TV shows. The media thrives on reinforcing negativity, for example, when people, especially famous people, aren't doing something well enough: who they have slept with, how terrible they look without makeup, how they have put on weight or lost weight, and so forth. Others love to read these stories. Gossiping about other people's inadequacies only reminds us of our own inadequacies, which, in turn, maintains a lower vibration rate in society at large. This is the complete opposite of what we need to be doing for each other. Gossip only helps to break people down. It is far more powerful for you and others to build people up. Imagine you had a night every week with your friends in which you were only allowed to compliment each other and talk about your dreams. Don't you think that would be a night you would look forward to?

Love is all accepting; it is kind and gentle, and it doesn't judge people. Begin to notice how you talk about yourself and others. You will be amazed at how good it makes you feel when you practice positive recognition. To do this for your children is a wonderful gift: a big smile will light up their faces when you do so. In my household, we used to have compliments every morning while sitting around the breakfast table. Each of us had a day that was our day for receiving and on that day the others would pay us one or two compliments. It was so much fun; the kids had to identify what they really liked about the other person because it had to be genuine. I loved it when it was my day because my children would tell me things that I didn't see in or about myself.

Am I doing a good enough job with my kids?

There was no way that I could possibly live up to my version of a perfect mother, and even now I am always striving to be a better mother. Every mother I know wants to be the best mother she can be. We all want to make sure that we give our children the opportunities they need to thrive and to do whatever makes them happy.

When my children started school, my vision included picking them up from school, helping with homework, watching their sports activities etc. As work expands, I have had to adjust this vision. Yet, I have learnt that my children grow with me. Whatever decision I make to follow my path in life, they embrace it. They may resist it at first because it represents change but we find ways of making it work. They still have their needs and want their time with me, but they don't necessarily need what I thought they needed. My children are a little bit older now; at 13, 11 and 9 they are quite self –sufficient. I share my hopes and dreams with them, and they are very supportive. I have realized that in my growing, in my stepping out and being myself in the world, being creative and following opportunities, I have given my children the opportunity to be independent.

Independence is one of the things I value in life; it is heart-warming, when I see my children displaying it. It has surprised me how confident and capable they have become, even at their young age. In my experience, I grow with my children; over time, I have made greater strides toward my dream life, but I also recognize how much I've chosen to limit myself along the way through my perceptions. I did know though, that as long as I was taking steps, learning more and having fun along the way, I could keep my sense of me as a person as well as a mother. Even before I knew my life direction, I felt I was constantly learning, and that, somehow, all of those things would come together.

Everyone in the house is allowed to make mistakes - including me. When I do, I apologize to my children and I tell them I made a mistake. In giving myself permission to make mistakes, my children see that it is also okay for them to make mistakes. Forgiveness goes a very long way in this world. It has been a harder journey to learn to forgive myself, to understand that it's okay for me to make mistakes and not be perfect – after all I am a Virgo! I want to experience the world from a place of love and compassion, understanding that we are all equal and that everyone has different dreams. Now I am more confident that I am doing a terrific job with my children and that we will grow and develop as a family as well as individuals as I move forward in my own path. I choose to acknowledge that I am amazing, because when I look at my children I see three incredible human beings. If we all could let go and forgive ourselves for our mistakes in life and understand that every one of us is an incredible human being, we would begin to open energetically to new and exciting possibilities.

How do I measure myself?

When looking in the mirror, we question if we are good enough, if we look good enough, if we're the right weight, or if our skin is looking too wrinkled. It is our choice how we perceive ourselves. We don't need to conform to anyone else's idea of who we should be. It is far more empowering to make "rules" that define our success and make us feel good. Every morning I write my intentions and priorities for the day in a diary. At the end the day, I reflect back and I write a list of my achievements and successes. Some days I won't complete all the priorities, but my focus is always on my successes. I go to bed feeling good about my day and who I was during that day. The more success I have each day, the better I feel about myself, and my overall perception becomes one of being successful.

In our attempts to discover a new direction in life we need to feel successful right now. We need to look at ourselves and know we are doing a terrific job and that we are on a journey. The more we embrace our journey and explore who we are, the faster we will achieve our goals. One way to acknowledge this is to write down those successes every day. If we constantly focus on the overall goal without acknowledging smaller goals and accomplishments along the way, it can feel like what we want is unachievable.

It doesn't matter what successes you choose to measure as long as it makes you feel good about what you're doing and you are happy. By focusing on every small success we bring more happiness into our lives because we feel good. This is true regardless of whether our decision is to go back into the workplace, start a new career, take up a hobby or continuing as an at-home mother. There is no right or wrong in life. It's about exploring life's possibilities and living from a place of love. Start being mindful about the way you measure yourself. Make sure that you win every day, that you see your day as a success, and that you see yourself as a success

Something will happen in your brain when you begin to focus on your successes in life. Your thoughts will shift to you being a success, and you will feel more successful. Given the way we send signals out into the universe, when we feel successful we create more confidence leading to further success. This one change can create an enormous difference to our attitude and our approach to life. When I started to see my story as successful rather than just as a story, an enormous change occurred in me. I felt better about myself, I opened up to opportunities and recognized what I had to offer the world. Now that my daily focus is on success, life feels more fun; it feels like I get more done and that I can achieve my bigger goals. Everyone has successes every day, regardless of who you are or what you do, because success is relative to what you measure it against. It has nothing to do with what the outside world determines you should be doing, whether you work, whether your children are number one in their class or the best basketball players in the team. It has everything to do with the way you look at life, what you think is important in your life, and the way that you measure success in your life.

I had a conversation with a friend who is a stay-at-home mother. She loves being a stay-at-home mother and she doesn't want to do anything else. Yet she feels that other people look at her as though she does not want enough out of life. If what you want is to be a stay-at-home mother and that makes you happy then be that person! It is no one else's business what we want to do with our lives. Equally *what other people think of us is none of our business*. When you measure your own success by what is important to you, it feels freeing. When you change the way you look at your life, and when you start looking at yourself in successful terms, you will feel better, more confident, and good things will happen that you did not expect.

What happened to me?

When I first had children, I had a clear picture of who I was and who I would be while they were growing up…but it all changed. I no longer wanted the things I used to think I wanted. I didn't want to be working full-time again – certainly not in a traditional 9-5 job. I realized that I wanted to express my happiness in life and to be creative. When my children came along and we were playful about creativity I could feel something opening up inside me. My vision had to change because I had become a different person.

The other thing that I experienced was the loss of "me" during those first few years in my children's lives. Suddenly I was washing every day, cleaning, cooking, mashing up food, making play dough and monitoring nap times. I was very blessed to be able to stay at home with my children during their early years, but I could feel my world shrinking. Having three children meant that the early childhood stage went on for years. Nine years passed between having my first child and having three children at school. In nine years we change a lot! We learn a lot about life, and we are not the same person as before we had children. Even though I studied during that time, my social life consisted largely of other mothers. As my world shrank, so did my confidence.

I was very blessed in that I was able to take some time out for the things I enjoyed, particularly early on with only one or two babies. I played golf for a couple of years and I wrote a book. I spent a limited time networking professionally, but on the whole I considered my role as the stay-at-home mother. When my youngest child was one year old I began studying life coaching, and that kept me sane for a while. I acquired some knowledge and learned some invaluable skills while making some incredible connections that were very sustaining at that time. Few of my friends had that opportunity, and they are now searching for what they want to do in the world. If that is you, know that, by reading this book, you are taking steps in your life! It is refreshing to consider our needs, wants and desires and bring them to the forefront of our lives; this is the perfect time to do so.

If you are already working and want to create some change because you don't enjoy your job, the hours you work, or you just want life to look a bit different, it is a matter of taking the time to develop your vision. Chapter 9 is dedicated to a discussion about time and priorities because I know the feeling of the constant juggling act to ensure that everything is done and everyone's needs are met. It is essential to value our own needs as well, which is one way to show love for ourselves. Give yourself permission and space to explore who you are and who you want to be. If we approach this from a purely time-based philosophy, we are not showing ourselves that love. Put more bluntly, if you truly love yourself, you can create some space to work on your own dreams and hopes.

Is love a verb or a feeling?

When we ask what love is, there is no doubt that we understand there is a feeling in our heart that we call love. I am not talking about sexual love; I am talking about genuine deep love from your heart, the type that is ever-expanding. When we had our children we didn't say, "I can only love my first child." As I had each of my children, the sheer love I felt for them was overwhelming, and I could feel my heart expanding rather than having to divide a finite amount of love inside.

Love is also something that we need actively to practice in our lives. I am constantly telling my children that I love them, but I am also constantly doing things for them to show them that I love them. That pertains to myself as well – I show myself love by doing little things for myself and prioritizing me. I love having a bath with oils and candles. It feels as though I am doing that for the love of me, to purely enjoy that moment and relax. When I am working from home, I might make myself a delicious salad for lunch because I know that I am nourishing my body. By doing these things I am setting a great example for my children because, when they are grown up, I want them to love themselves and show themselves that love.

The more you can move into that feeling of loving, the more you will connect and begin to understand what you want to get out of your life. Feeling that love consistently in our life may mean that we need to change the way we think about things and what we are doing. Love and accept who you are now, even if you know you want to change.

The saying that "life is a journey" is true, but you don't have to reach any particular destination in this lifetime. When I achieve goals in my life, I don't say, "Wow, that's it, I'm finished." I celebrate and look at what else I want to work towards in my bigger dream and, importantly, I notice who I am becoming along that journey. The beauty of life is that you choose your goals, but then don't get caught up on having to achieve those goals in a certain timeframe.

Repetitive … maybe, but some things we need to hear more than once! Our job is to be happy on our journey and accept all the things that come along the way, treat them with love as learning opportunities, and love ourselves through it all. Let go and live from a place of no resistance, from a place of love, not fear, and choose the journey that you want. Life does not just happen to us; it is not random. Rather, it is based upon our choices; it can be fun, vibrant and exciting, or it can be dull, dreary and boring. It will be whatever you choose and whatever feeling you choose to have along the journey. It is pointless to reach a huge life goal if you are feeling miserable all the way to achieving it.

Being true to the "inner me"

Part of loving ourselves and being happy means we must feel in alignment with whatever we are doing with our lives. Whatever our goals and dreams are, they must feel good inside at that core level of who we are. I know how, in my role as a mother, it can be quite difficult to make time to explore that side of myself, but it is something I must prioritize. I want to be sure my actions are moving me toward who I want to be; and my inner self knows if I am on track. One thing I needed to clarify in my life was that there is an inner self that at times was not always reflected in my actions. That discord was very uncomfortable to live in because I knew I wasn't being who I wanted to be.

Now that I am doing what I really want, I feel a sense of peace about whom I am. But I had to take time to find myself. In fact, the bigger picture is still evolving for me. Taking time, writing, answering questions, exploring and working on my thoughts and beliefs, have contributed to me getting in touch with my inner self. I used to judge myself because I thought what I wanted was unreasonable. Instead of embracing my dreams, I put them aside. When we recognize that we are doing that, it is time to step up and say, "I have something that I want to do in this life." This might sound logical, yet so many people never become who they want to be. We can avoid making decisions and just passively follow what seems a "normal" path in life, but that does not move us closer to our dreams and who we want to be. Decisions feel better when they're in alignment with that inner spirit that wants to shine.

Do I need to create inner change?

No one is forced to create inner change. There's no need for it if you are 100% happy with who you are and where you're headed. If you are content with your health, social circles, relationships and finances, then you don't need to change. For most people though, life doesn't look the way they want. If that is true for you, then, yes, you need to change.

Inner change means changing our thoughts, feelings, attitudes and dreams. When we explore these concepts and how we operate in the world, we can start to see where changes are needed. Many of us resist change vehemently, even though we might like some things to be different. I had nine years living with babies, toddlers or young children. The world I was comfortable in was a children's world. I knew about school because my eldest was at school while my youngest was still at home. But I didn't know what was next for me, and I didn't know what I wanted that change to look like.

It can be confronting to know that you want to change but being unsure of what that change looks like. In theory, there were definitely some parts of my life that I wanted to change, but in reality there were things I enjoyed about life as it was. In my vision, I wasn't sure how to hang onto the things I did not want to lose, such as the relationship with my children and the time I was able to spend with them. I wasn't going to sacrifice those to ensure that my vision came true. This kept me running around in circles. What I needed to do was to clarify my vision – to focus on how I wanted to feel as well and what I wanted to have in my life. I had to learn to observe if my thinking and feeling were supporting my dreams. Frankly, neither was supportive of the direction I wanted to move into, so inner change was necessary before I took action. Once that inner change was made then the actions were inspired and came easily.

The effect of judgment

We love to judge ourselves as well as judging others. I can be my own harshest critic about my body, the way I'm being a mother, whether I get enough done in a day or where I am in life. In the end, I know that if I judge myself as not being good enough, I feel horrible. When we judge others, it immediately puts a barrier in our relationship. We can feel it in the relationship with our children; when we judge them, there is a feeling of disconnect. I want them to know that I love them unconditionally and to feel safe about making mistakes. But I want that for myself too; I want experience that kindness and loving compassion, to turn the love I have for other people toward myself and experience that same kind of love.

When I began to learn about judgment and the effect it had on my life, I was quite shocked because we are taught to judge from a young age. We tend to judge everything as good or bad instead of accepting things as situations in our life. When one particular relationship ended for me, I considered it a disaster. However, a few months later things happened, revealing that this was by far the best possible outcome for me personally. But I couldn't see it at the time. Again, this was purely because of the judgment that I held around the situation. If I had had been able to approach it with love, knowing it would all turn out, I wouldn't have needed to go through all those negative emotions.

Every time we judge ourselves, or focus on what is wrong with us rather than what's right with us, we are not showing self-love. Self-love means we love our self where we are right now, knowing that we are in a process of growing. As we proceed through this time of self-discovery, we learn to love ourselves through experience. The more we can love, the higher our vibration will be, meaning we can open up more possibilities to explore. If we continually judge ourselves for where we are or the way we look, we are focusing on the things we don't want. *If you want change, you must focus on what you want and do so from a loving perspective.*

How do I love myself right now, if I see things I need to change?

Loving oneself is a big challenge for many people. Remember, love is both a verb and a feeling. Love is something we can practice. The more we practice, the better we become at it. Feeling love is something that we do from our hearts, not from our heads. When we think loving thoughts, we will feel the love in our heart. It is so easy to say, "You must love yourself," but sometimes that feels very hard to do. If you can master how you think and feel, you can create anything. Practicing love means we have patience, we smile a lot, we forgive ourselves, and we choose to look at situations and people with love.

How do I find what I am passionate about?

This is almost the crux of what we ask ourselves, especially once our children are at school. I know that I want something more, but how do I decide what that is? We can start by looking at what we are passionate about now. When considering what you're passionate about, stop worrying about whether it is right, wrong, good, bad, too big or too small. It's totally up to you what you want have and experience in this lifetime. The beauty of being human is that this is different for each of us. We each have skills, talents and experiences that form our unique perspective on the world. It is what makes life interesting. Deep down, only you can know what you are passionate about.

Passion feels good in your heart. I had an inkling about my passions when my children began school. I knew vaguely that it involved helping people in some way, and that I wanted to see people inspired and motivated. My vision has matured over a number of years; it includes people feeling love for themselves and seeing the world as a beautiful place. I know the power of seeing the world from this perspective, but it took time to realize that others see the world differently. I know that love is the driving force in the world; and at a personal level, it makes a huge difference actually to live it.

As you embark on your journey of self-discovery bring as much love into your life as you can. Practice it daily, for it can lighten everything and open possibilities beyond your wildest dreams. It does not matter who you are right now, or what your living situation is – when you commit to bringing more love into your world, life will change. You don't need to know how things will work out or how to incorporate your passion into your life. All you need to work on is rediscovering that passionate feeling. Looking back at when I was a child, I was always attracted to people and wanted them to feel good. I'm sure this comes from the unconscious core of wanting to love myself. Life has taken me on such a beautiful journey starting from not loving myself and having to learn this. I now know what self-love feels like and that it makes an extraordinary difference to life. It changes your actions, what you tolerate, your dreams and what you think you deserve.

Needing others to change

This is another of the biggest misconceptions in our society that keeps us from reaching our potential. If we think we need anything from anyone else at any time, we are disempowered. We become victim to circumstance. I often hear people say, "When my husband has a new job…" or "when the children are settled…" Many people hand over their happiness and rely on someone else to change for them to be happy. Life doesn't work that way. *It is our responsibility to be happy regardless of what anyone else is doing.*

If we think we need someone else to change something in order to get time, then that is the experience we will create. If WE decide to prioritize ourselves, we will make the time. It is not up to anybody else to change our life. Our job is to look after ourselves, to love us and be happy now. As mothers, one of our jobs is to look after our children physically, emotionally, mentally and spiritually. However, it is also our responsibility to create the life we want. There are practicalities associated with looking after children, but don't allow yourself to be locked into any story or any boundaries of what you can and can't do. If we choose to think that way, we hold ourselves back from seeing opportunities and reaching our full potential. We create excuses for why we can't do something rather than for why we can do something.

There are myriads of inspiring people in the world who overcome all sorts of obstacles and challenges in their lives. We do not have to succumb to thinking that we can't do anything because we have children. Equally, we do not have to succumb to thinking that we have to do anything other than being a mother. We can choose to feel empowered. Remember, you don't have to know how things will work out; start with a vision. Don't let any excuses stand in your way. If there is something that you want to do, then life will find a way to help you to achieve it. If you don't know what that is yet, feel good knowing that you are on a journey. Make some time to discover what it is you want to do. Don't get sucked into routines and habits that keep you feeling small or incapable. I know in my heart that anyone can do anything.

Chapter Summary

Love is the highest vibrational force in the universe and it can completely change lives. Every person has a right to feel love and loved. By living from a place of love you will naturally feel happier, healthier and appreciate more in your life. If you continually compare yourself to others and judge yourself as better or worse than them, you are not living from love. When you can love yourself, you have more courage to show yourself to the world; it is an extraordinary gift to give your children as it gives them permission to do the same.

We all have a story of our life and we can choose to speak of this in a positive or a negative light. The story does not define us; it is who we become as we are in the story. When you speak of your past, do so from a perspective of success; see how amazing you truly are in the path you have chosen thus far. We can all choose to see our life as successful –we are just not practiced at doing so. When you decide to create "rules" for measuring your success, you begin to think and feel differently.

Having children can feel like our world is shrinking. What we thought we wanted most often changes and it can leave us feeling unsure of what we really want. The more we spend time with the "inner me," the more we can work out what will make our heart sing. If we continue to plod along life doing the things that need to be done, without consideration of what makes us happy, we will remain stagnant. We can embark on our life journey with zest and excitement, or we can make it dull and dreary. If we focus on our "wrongs" instead on our "rights", we feel bad. We all need to love ourselves now, even knowing that we want to change. In fact, the more we love ourselves, the faster any change can occur.

Passion is an expression of love. To feel love more fully, we ideally want to spend our days doing things we are passionate about. We all have passion in our heart, but we may have stifled it for so long we no longer recognize it. This is why we need to get in tune with that "inner me," so we can rediscover that passion. If you feel you need others to change in order for you to follow your bliss, then you are disempowering yourself. You may not know how your dreams will become reality, but needing anyone else to change before you can achieve it means you are handing over your power to someone else. Many thoughts that limit us are simply beliefs that can be changed. When you operate solely from love for you, your family and others in the world, you will discover that anything is possible.

Questions for self-reflection

1. What successes have I had in my life? Make a list.

_____

_____

_____

_____

_____

2. What do I need to forgive myself for?

_____

_____

_____

_____

3. What is one thing I can do to love myself better?

_____

_____

_____

_____

_____

CHAPTER 4

KNOWING WHAT YOU WANT

So many people drift along in life, wanting something
more but not knowing what. To fulfill our potential we
must have a clear vision of what that looks like for us.
The better we know it, the more we will recognize it.

A while ago, a beautiful friend and her three daughters were killed in a horrific house fire, and the father/husband was in hospital fighting for his life. It left our community absolutely shattered. This was absolutely devastating for my children as well as for the group of children who were all very close friends with the girls. When it happened, no one really knew what to do. The only thing I knew was that I wanted to help my children find a way to move through this and find joy in life again.

I called the mothers of the victims' friends and we held a meeting at my home. I proposed to the children that we fundraise to help the father in his situation. There was nothing else we could have done at that time, and we knew that he would have to begin his life all over again. The children came up with lots of creative ideas of what they would like to do. We narrowed these down and settled on organizing a raffle and a tribute concert – the three young girls had always loved music and dancing.

The children initially set themselves the target of raising $5,000. This was a lot of money to a group of 10-and 11-year-old children, but they were very determined. We didn't know how things were going to work out, but we knew what we all wanted. Over the next few weeks, we watched these children approach local businesses requesting prizes for the raffle. The response was overwhelming. Within four weeks they had obtained prizes worth over $20,000 with an incredible level of support from the local community. As the project grew, we asked our local Lions Club to help us obtain a raffle license. The children focused so much loving energy on this project that the outcome could only be good. It felt like working two full-time jobs managing the raffle and also organizing the concert in the background. However, within four months, these children managed to raise over $42,000.

The concert, an incredible display of dance and music, ran for 4 ½ hours without costing a cent. We knew just how much the girls would have loved it. Every performer, the light-and-sound technicians and the caterer all donated their time to that event. To watch our children stand up and sing at that concert, with smiles on their faces, remembering these girls we had all loved, was an extraordinary moment for everyone involved. That project was a significant turning point for my children – they saw that they were able to create something good out of a devastating situation. I knew that our project had been so filled with love there was no chance for it to fail. But I also remember how much I wanted to help our children and the father in any way that we could. What then transpired through the vision and determination was a miracle. Obviously in that particular situation there was a catalyst to knowing what I wanted … life isn't always so clear.

What do I really want?

Many of us have hopes and dreams residing in the back of our minds, but we may not have defined them completely. We move with the flow of life, and every now and then a thought will cross our mind about something we might prefer to be different. Taking the time to think about what you want out of life is giving yourself a gift. Although the world can appear entirely materialistic, many of us were taught not to want the material "stuff." Whatever you want is Ok! At the same time, realize that *whatever it is you want, it is because of the feeling you think it will give you when you achieve it.* It is not about material stuff or the work we want to do, but about the fact that we want to feel happy and secure. Knowing that means you can start bringing those feelings into your life right now.

Unless we define what we want, we can't move towards it. We tend to be very clear and able to describe what we don't want. If we focus on, and talk about, what we don't want, we will create more of that. It is far more beneficial to define what you want and start working toward that! If you find it difficult to define what you want, start by writing a list of the things you don't want. Once you've done that, use each item on your list to clarify what you do want by asking yourself "So what do I want?" You can use this approach for defining anything – health, finances, relationships and the material things. Let your imagination run wild! We have been taught to think small. We have beliefs that make us think that what we want is not realistic or we can't possibly achieve it, rather than being open to any opportunities or to making a decision about what we really want.

Knowing what we want may mean defining some material things, like the kind of house we want to live in, what car we want to drive, where we want to live, what kind of furniture we want, what kind of food we want to eat, what sort of friends we want to have in our lives, what kind of relationships we want, how we want our bodies to look and feel etc. These all encompass the things we want in life. I love to look at houses and cars that I like. I don't know when they will come into my life, but it's fun to look, touch and play with that idea. I understand that the more I am doing that, the more the universe is shifting things so they can come into my life.

As a mother, there are important things I want for my children such as health, happiness, confidence etc. My top priority is to have loving, connected relationships with them. Other things I want do not exclude my children. The vision for my life includes them as well as a plethora of other people and things. It is only now that I have started to define what I really want and I hold that vision as I take steps towards achieving it, that things are falling into place. If you don't know what you want, take some time out to define it. Start with the material things and know that if you are not really sure now, at some point as you embark on this path, clarity will come.

Whatever I want…

Henry Ford said, "*Whether you think you can or you think you can't, either way you are right.*" Our thinking and beliefs influence our outcomes. Life hands us experiences that mirror our beliefs. Everyone has fears and beliefs that aren't serving them. When I embarked on the fundraising project, I didn't know how it would evolve. I knew deep down in my heart that we could achieve what we wanted, but there were moments when I didn't know how it would all come together. We stayed focused and positive and in the end the outcome was extraordinary! If you think you can't have what you truly desire, it's time to examine what beliefs or fears are holding you back.

What does fulfillment feel like?

This is so different for everyone. When we stop worrying about whether other people approve of us or feel the same way as we do, we can connect with our heart's true desire. Your job is to determine what fulfills you. When I became a mother, it was very fulfilling to be able to hold this beautiful little person and to know that I could give her what she needed. As my children grew and went to school, that changed. It is still fulfilling to be with my children and to see them grow and develop, but there's something more that I want in my life. For me, but probably not for everyone, that includes an element of work. It is about whatever makes you happy, whatever makes you feel good.

It is important that we know what fulfillment feels like so we can bring more of it into our life. There's a little place inside us that tingles with joy and the satisfaction in what we are doing. If you don't know or remember that feeling, look back on your life and recall those moments. Normally it's when we feel that pure joy and excitement of being in the moment, and not worrying or thinking about anything other than what we are doing. We were not judging whether we had done a good enough job, whether we were right or wrong or whether we were too big or too small. We were content in that moment and felt fulfilled. Fulfillment might mean cooking a delicious meal for your family, reading at school in your child's classroom or giving a talk to thousands of people. It doesn't matter what it is, only that you understand what is fulfilling for you. The better you know yourself, the more you know what will bring the feeling of fulfillment into your life. When my children were born, I felt frumpy because I was carrying extra weight, and I was so tired from night feeds. I didn't feel much like a woman, although ironically, you are as feminine as you can get in that situation. Now when I look in the mirror, I see a woman who wants to feel feminine and who has hopes and dreams that include her children without them limiting her.

Do my beliefs get in the way of my dreams?

Absolutely, they do! Sometimes those beliefs don't even allow us to dream or set goals. All the experiences associated with creating limiting beliefs made us forget that we could do anything and that the world offers us an abundance of opportunities. We narrow things down to what feels realistic and what we think could fit into our life. Every mother I have spoken with wants to make sure her children have the best opportunities in life and takes this into consideration when following her own path. It is only recently that I have had the courage to get out of my own way and get clear about my dreams. Those dreams and possibilities had become smaller and smaller over the years, particularly while I was at home being a mother to my young children. Children are time-consuming and my whole life was entirely dedicated to them for many years. During that time, the world seemed to get smaller and I forgot there were dreams I had…because life got in the way.

I now know that it is essential for us to dream. Beginning to dream again has been an ongoing process for me. Each week as I write my dreams down, I find they continue to expand. As I grow and see more possibilities, my dreams also grow. I ask myself, "What would I be, do or have if I could have anything?" Your answers to this question will show you where your thinking is right now and how much it could expand. If you have narrowed your hopes and dreams because you believe that you can't achieve them, answering this question can help your imagination expand.

We never let go of our life dream, of the vision we want to realize in our life. It is the big picture, not the next goal we want to achieve. I have some very lofty dreams now that excite me. I am thrilled by the thought of bringing these dreams into my life. I don't know how, but it is exciting to dream again and to move away from the beliefs that I had about what life is going to be for me. I know now that my beliefs influenced my life greatly in the past few years. Getting back in touch with my dreams has truly helped me expand my awareness of myself and of my possibilities.

The art of dreaming

Remember when you were a child and you could do anything or be anyone? I watch my 9-year-old son playing outside with a stick – he might be a soldier fighting one moment and the next he's an astronaut charging to the moon. When he's playing, he is that person he's imagining and he is practicing of the art of dreaming. He doesn't say to himself, "I can't be that person in this lifetime, so I won't play." He just gets out there and plays. He has so much fun and doesn't need anyone else around him to play. That's what the art of dreaming is about. It's getting back to your spirit, to what you truly love and what is fun. Dreaming is an art that easily opens up to joy and possibilities.

Dreaming is supposed to be fun! I have so much fun dreaming about the things I want. I can picture myself in the dream and run it like a movie. I know that the vibration this sends into the universe is helping to create and to make those dreams come true. It is so exciting to be in that moment and to dedicate some time to dreaming. At the same time we need to balance being in the present moment and enjoy ourselves as well!

Do be mindful about the people with whom you choose to share your dreams; you want to be sure that they also hold that dream for you. There are people around who will knock you or your dream down and fill you with doubt. You want to be clear in your dream process to let go of any inhibitions and limiting beliefs and move into a space of thinking and dreaming about what you really want. This may mean you need to keep that vision to yourself or only share it with a few people – only those who you trust and whom you know will support you in that dream. Dreaming is about having fun. Be playful with it; allow it to open up your mind and your heart again and allow your dreams to start guiding what you are going to do next in your life. When you dream, do so from your heart and spirit; as you are doing that, you are going to get in touch with what you are passionate about.

Are they really your dreams?

When we are dreaming about what we want in our life, we are free to decide precisely what we want. Although we may not realize it, there are so many influences that can affect these dreams – what we were told by our parents, our friends, family, even societal expectations. It seems everyone around us has an opinion about what we should or shouldn't do. This can mean that we lose sight of whether our dream is actually ours or if belongs to someone else. If you are not motivated and inspired by those dreams, it could be worth checking to make sure they are in alignment with what you really want.

We do not intend to let go of our dreams; this tends to happen as a subconscious level over time as we listen to other people and try to please others. Women especially, spend a lot of time pleasing others. In doing so we can lose sight of what the dream is for us. I can't stress it enough – our dreams must be in alignment with the person we want to be. We don't want to end up dying with our dream still inside. If there are things in your life that you want to do, then have courage and allow them to blossom. Make sure that whatever you think you want is yours and not what anyone else is saying that you want. Don't be swayed by the media or by what other people say. Stay true to your heart and be very clear about that dream of yours.

What's my vision?

Your vision is what you imagine life looks like both on the journey towards and when you reach your dream. You might like to break that down to the basics of family, friends, health, finances, community, home, spirituality, fun, romance, career – any category that you like and that feels good for you. There's no right or wrong there. Creating such a vision should be an enjoyable process.

Allow all things you want to be included in your vision even if you don't know how they will come about. Make sure that it feels good; that in some small way it perhaps even feels possible. Remember you don't have to know how it will happen, just create the vision of what you really want. If your vision feels completely out of reach, just keep it as part of your bigger life dream, then bring your focus back onto something that you believe is possible. But don't ever give up on that big dream. When you know that you are working toward a bigger dream, each step will come into focus along the way. Rather than concentrating on what you can do right now while the kids are at school, start to look at a bigger picture of yourself and your life. Know that as your vision expands and as you begin to experience small successes along the way, your ability to believe in the bigger things will also expand. That feeling of success will grow within you as you define and refine your vision.

If I could do anything and knew I wouldn't fail, I would...

This is a wonderful exercise that anyone can do to open his or her mind. Take a piece of blank paper and at the top write "If I could do anything and knew I wouldn't fail, I would ..." Then let go and dream of possibilities. Allow your heart and mind to open and expand. Would you travel the world, become a motivational speaker or climb Mount Everest? The more you expand your dreams and your mind, the more fun you can have, even if your ideas seem ridiculous right now. When I look at my dream list, I have no idea how a lot of things are going to come into being. But I know that, the better I feel about them, the more my energy expands into the universe to help me create those things.

When I first did this exercise I found it quite difficult because I had limited my thinking. I began thinking of things that seemed sensible and could fit in with my life. The more I did this exercise, the more I allowed new and adventurous ideas to open up. As long as I feel good when I look at those things, I know that that the possibility exists for them to come into my reality. The aim of this exercise is purely to open up your energy and expand the possibilities you see for your life.

What if my vision and dreams conflict with the kids?

My vision for life includes my children, but I don't have a clear picture yet of how it all fits together. I just know that it will work somehow because ultimately, that is what I want. If your vision feels like it conflicts with the children, you are probably worrying about how things might happen. Don't worry about that; just concentrate on your dream.

Remember, your life dream might come to fruition in 10, 20, even 30 years. If you are passionate about your dream, you can be content knowing that the work you are doing now is moving you closer to that dream. For me, I am very happy now with a dream inside and knowing that everything I am doing contributes to that dream. I have stopped worrying about whether I will have time to do all things I want to do; I just hold my vision knowing that, at some point, it will all work out.

How can I make my dreams come true?

We have been conditioned to believe we have some control over the way things happen. Yet, we only have control over our response to situations. Having control is different from influencing the outcomes. Our energy definitely influences what we create but it does not control it. We don't know how things will happen although we might have ideas and expectations. When situations don't look the way we expect, we tend to judge them negatively rather than realizing there is a bigger plan. For example, we may decide we want to earn more money but then we lose our job. That looks terrible, but if we could see that another, better paying job waits around the corner we would not need to worry.

Life rarely goes according to our own plan. Our vision will be more powerful if we can let go of needing to know how things will happen. Once we begin to take deliberate steps, events and experiences guide us. The cliché "we don't know what we don't know"' is true! We need to know that somehow things will happen and will fall into place. Inevitably, if we focus on the "how" we will be tempted to make our dreams smaller. Over time, the effect of this can damage your spirit ever so slightly. Instead, work on removing any doubt and worry about how it will happen. Allow something bigger than yourself to enter your life and create the desired transformation that will bring what you want.

When I was working on the project with the children, we decided that we wanted to contact a world famous singer (name deliberately withheld) to ask her to support our cause. We had no idea of how we would contact her; we just knew that we wanted to make contact. My children hand wrote a beautiful letter explaining the situation and putting their request into words. We had no idea of how we would get that letter to the singer but we felt it wasn't worth sending it to her managers because it probably wouldn't get through their screening processes. A couple of days later, one of the mothers involved in the project was collecting a raffle prize from a local business and mentioned our letter. She was asked, "How are you getting the letter to the singer?" It turned out she knew someone who knew someone who could get this letter directly to the singer. There is no way we could have planned that! We emailed the letter to our contact who forwarded it through the chain to the singer. Not surprisingly, she was unavailable for the concert, but she very graciously sent us some signed merchandise to use in an auction. The children were very excited, experiencing the tangible evidence of a situation with an unpredictable outcome, but in which we all simply held the vision.

Let go and allow…

Letting go basically means that we stop worrying about HOW something will happen, and in doing so we let go of any resistance. Instead we move into a space of allowing. When we wrote the letter to the singer, we just knew it would reach her. We didn't panic or search around the Internet. We wrote the letter and said, "Please show us how" because we know this feels right. And of course, everything lined up.

When we stop doubting ourselves and tune in to our intuition about what our next step is, we can move with confidence in the direction of our dreams. We can choose to believe in our self and take small steps, which will start to bring that dream toward us. It's like a sort of invisible magic. However, if we doubt and are unsure of whether our dreams can happen, we push them further away. If we follow the natural steps that our intuition tells us, even if they don't make sense, then we are moving to where we are meant to be. Letting go and allowing is really about us getting out of our own way and stop trying to control everything. It doesn't matter how big the dream is – you can have it. When you are in that place of working out what you want in your life, as you rediscover who you want to be, do not be limited by false beliefs. If your idea fills your heart with joy, include it in your dream. This is what life is about, so stop worrying about how things will happen and allow your spirit to shine through.

Chapter Summary

Most people are fairly clear about what they don't want in life, but they are unsure when it comes to defining what they truly want. Many who do define what they want aim too small because they have limited their vision so much they can't see any bigger possibilities. Unless we have a vision, we cannot reach any goals or dreams. Instead, we succumb to floating through life thinking things happen to us.

Thinking small is a syndrome that affects many people. It is disempowering and only serves to limit our dreams. Everyone is driven by beliefs, and most of the time those beliefs tell us we can't be, do or have what we want; we should "get real," or be serious about what we want. Every one of our beliefs can and should be questioned to determine its validity. If your life does not look that way you want, you have beliefs that are holding you back.

Dreaming plays a huge role in defining what we want. When we were children, it was easy and natural to dream, but as we entered school, we were told to stop dreaming and focus on what we were doing. This led to confusion about the role of dreaming and thoughts that it was mostly something children did. To create the vision of the life you want, dreaming is essential. Always make sure your dreams make your heart sing and are not other people's ideas of what you should do.

Our vision is supposed to expand constantly. As you dream more, you grow into them and find you need to think bigger again. Let go and have fun playing with your imagination of what is possible for you. Make sure your vision is in alignment with what your heart desires, not what you think you should want.

If you focus on "how" anything will come about in this world, you immediately limit yourself because you don't know the how. As you begin to design your vision, you might be concerned that it won't fit in with the children…this is because you are worried about the how. Just get out of the way and have fun imagining what you want.

Allowing our dreams means we need to allow them to develop fully into a vision that is in alignment with us as well as letting go of any resistance. It does not mean just letting go and taking no action. It does mean stop worrying about how anything will occur and look for the magic of the universe to help make things happen.

Questions for self-reflection

1. What do I really want in life? Break it down to family, friends, health, finances, career, community, spirituality.

_____

_____

_____

_____

_____

2. If I could do anything and knew I couldn't fail, I would ...

_____

_____

_____

_____

_____

3. What can I do to let go more and allow my dreams to come into fruition?

_____

_____

_____

_____

_____

CHAPTER 5

LISTENING TO YOUR HEART

All of the answers to our questions in life are stored in our heart. If we could stop the busyness and listen we would find the direction we are seeking.

Several years ago I found myself at a point where I was not feeling very happy about my life, who I was, or where my life was going. My husband David and I had bought a business together. It was a retail store in an industry that was clearly going downhill. Nine months after we bought the store, David was diagnosed with B-cell Lymphoma, a type of cancer of the blood. It was a tumultuous time during which David went through chemotherapy and blood transfusions to get him back to health. During this time I realized how unhappy I had become in my marriage. I felt it wasn't the right time to make decisions because David was so sick and needed to focus on getting well, and we had three young children. I really did not know what to do.

At some point during his treatment I stopped and listened to my heart. I knew I could not go on in my marriage anymore, which was devastating for me. My parents had divorced when I was young and I always believed I would never do that. I wanted my kids to have both their parents around. However, in my heart I really wasn't happy, through no fault of David's or of my own. The marriage simply wasn't working anymore. So when David improved to the point at which we knew he was on his way to being all clear and his chemotherapy treatments were finished, I told him that I believed we needed to separate. It was one of the most difficult conversations I've ever had in my life. David is a lovely man and I didn't want to hurt him.

In my head I had a list of all the reasons why I needed to stay, but I simply knew that it wasn't to be. So I embarked on a journey that I totally had not expected. At the same time, this journey has revealed some incredible strengths in me, and it has allowed me the opportunity to open up to life in a different way. David and I are still friends and we have family time with our children, although it doesn't happen very often anymore as he lives a long way away from us. But when we do get together, the kids really enjoy it and we all have a good time. I know divorce and relationships are a tricky topic and every case is different. I knew in my heart at the time that it was the right decision for me. I share this story not to encourage anyone to get divorced, but to encourage people to listen to what their heart is saying, because a lot of times we get caught up in what we think and we don't follow our heart. Generally speaking, if we follow our heart we will be happier.

The energy field of the heart

When we think of the heart, we think of an organ that pumps blood around our body. Those of you who know more about energy might think of the heart chakra or of the heart as the place of feelings. If you ask someone to point to themselves, most likely they will point to their heart area. It seems we naturally sense that the heart is an area of importance.

What few people realize, though, is that the heart contains it's own brain that communicates and interacts with the head brain. In 1991 Dr. J. Andrew Armour introduced the term "heart brain". Research from the Heartmath Institute explains that the heart is an intricate network of several types of neurons, neurotransmitters, protein and support cells like those found in the head brain. The head-brain and heart-brain are constantly communicating with each other.

When our heart maintains a stable rhythm, it has greater influence over the head-brain and we see benefits such as greater mental clarity and intuitive ability. This means if we focus our attention on the heart area, we can pro-actively create changes in our head-brain functions.

The heart generates the largest electromagnetic field in the body. It is up to 60 times stronger than the head brain. Scientific research is ongoing to discover more about the heart and the energy it sends out. For now, remember, our thoughts help to create our feelings, and our feelings are sending the vibrations out to the universe. So the better you feel about yourself, the more you will find yourself in circumstances that reflect your good feelings.

Why do we get stuck in our head?

"The intuitive mind is a sacred gift and the rational mind is a faithful servant. We have created a society that honors the servant and has forgotten the gift."

Albert Einstein

We try to make sense of the world by thinking about it. We are taught this, and it is inherent in us as we learn to perceive the world we live in. At any point in time, there are many more stimuli impacting on us than we can possibly process, so we learn to select the stimuli to which we want to pay attention, which means we also learn to exclude a lot of stimuli that are irrelevant to us. We try to use logic and rationalize events that occur in life, all of which is done in our head. At one level, for a variety of reasons, it might have made sense for me to stay in my marriage, but in my heart, I wasn't happy and so I knew I needed to act even if I didn't know how things would work out. Ultimately, I wanted to be happy and knew that was going to happen in the situation I was in.

When our heart tells us something, it's natural to try to make sense of it logically. We like to be able to explain why we make a particular decision. Many times the message we intuit in our heart makes no logical sense. Attempts to impose logic create confusion for us; it can make us doubt that we are making the right decision. Of course, thinking does have its place in this world as well! I am referring to decisions such as what we want in life, the kinds of friends we want to be around and how best to parent our children. Listening to what our head is telling us might lead to a very different answer than when listening to our heart. When we follow our heart instead of taking action because it appears to make more sense, we generally feel happier and more satisfied. Remember, the heart also represents love, so when we start to make more decisions from a place of love rather than from sheer logic, our decisions affect our lives much more positively.

What does whole brain utilization mean?

Our brain is divided into a left and a right hemisphere. Each hemisphere has specialized functions - the left hemisphere is used for logic, order, sequence and language, and the right hemisphere is the center of our creativity where we interpret symbols, pictures and music. It is a common misunderstanding that we only use 5% of our brain capacity. In truth, we have the ability to and do use all of our brain. Different parts of our brain are used for different bodily functions. If parts of our brain don't work, one or more of our body functions wouldn't work either.

We have the option to use our brain more effectively, however, such as integrating the use of our left and right brain. There are activities we can do to stimulate both sides of the brain to ensure that both sides of our brains are switched on. These are especially good to use with children in the mornings before school. Two of my favorites are:

- Cross crawl march: when your right foot is forward, your left arm is up and when your left foot is forward, your right arm is up. You can march around the room or on the spot. As our left and right sides of the body are controlled by different sides in the brain this exercise helps to activate the whole brain.
- The lazy 8: hold your arms straight out in front of you and wave them in the shape of an 8 on the side ∞ (an infinity sign). Again the crossover motion helps to engage the entire brain.

What we achieve in life begins with intention, and even the use of our brain is affected by our intentions. If your intention is to use your whole brain, then you can do it very simply. The two exercises above will certainly help to make you feel like you are engaging the whole brain.

You already know!

I believe everyone implicitly know the answers to their life concerning what is best for them. The point really is whether we trust those answers. We are used to making decisions from the head, decisions that seem logical. Yet, we always have the option of listening to our heart. At times, it can be difficult to trust the answers from our heart because they don't always make sense. During the time we were going through our divorce, many thoughts did not make any sense. Yet I knew implicitly that the decision to divorce would make me happier in the long term. While the divorce certainly brought challenges, I still feel it was the right decision regardless of what life might have looked like otherwise.

People tend to want confirmation that they are on the right track and that their decisions coming from the heart are "correct". It is much easier to follow a path that makes sense in both your head and your heart. Wanting confirmation comes back to us wanting to control the way things occur in our lives because we feel safer. The beautiful thing about our heart is that it is essentially an inbuilt emotional guidance system that tells us if we are on the right track. When we are not feeling good or happy, we know that something is not right in our lives. From a decision-making perspective, we know that, if it doesn't feel good, it's probably not the time to do it.

When we are pondering our life's purpose or what to do next, our heart knows and it will give us an answer. But then we try to rationalize the message to make sure it's actually the right answer! It does not work that way; our purpose, decisions and possibilities don't always make sense to us because we don't have the full picture. That is, we don't know everything. Outcomes of decisions made from the heart are generally far better for us than decisions based purely on thinking. By letting go of any expected outcomes, we open ourselves to the possibility that other outcomes may serve us better and provide us with a better experience. Life becomes easier when we believe that whatever happens is the right thing for us.

The next step is to determine who we are becoming now that we are no longer who we thought we would be. You might like to read that twice! Your priorities definitely change once you become a mother. With the acceptance that your priorities have changed and the knowledge that you are now entering a different stage of life, you have the opportunity to reconnect with your spirit for answers. If you can get back in tune with what your heart is telling you, you can begin to develop your vision and create the life you will love.

What's most important to you?

When asked what is most important to us, most mothers naturally mention the relationship with their children or with others, but it is equally important to identify your own needs as a woman and as a person. Taking time to reflect on who we are, what we bring to this world and what we want out of this life, is a gift to ourselves. Once you know what is important to you, you begin to define your path more clearly; you become more creative about your life. Whatever is important to you and the direction you choose to take is neither right nor wrong as long as it makes sense to you emotionally. Being happy and following your heart is the only important thing; it makes you an outstanding role model for everyone!

You may get conflicting views from your partner or friends who have other ideas about what you should want. If you know in your heart what you want, but others are trying to suppress that, realize that you give away some of your power if you listen to them. You have the answers in you, and you don't need to listen or consult with anyone to make sure that you are on the right track. Everyone's life path is unique – some of your friends will want to stay at home, some will want to take up a hobby or a sport, and others will want to go back to the workplace. When you embark on changes, some people around you will resist it because they are familiar and comfortable with the role you play in their life. They may feel threatened as you change because they can feel the relationship changing. They may feel forced to review their relationship with you and even review their own life. If what you want differs from what others around you believe you should want, it may take more tenacity to create change.

The mirror effect

The mirror effect shows us that everything in our life is a mirror of us, a reflection of our deepest beliefs. Many things in my marriage were reflected back to me that I did not like or understand at the time. Looking back, however, I can see that I helped to create the events that were occurring. I could not blame David for everything that was going wrong – it was most definitely a reflection of what I believed at that time.

When something occurs that we don't like, it provides an opportunity to gain clarity about what's happening at our deepest level. It's one of the reasons that life is so perfect. If we could understand that every situation mirrors something in us, it should help us to realize what we need to change. When we don't get what we want, there is a vibrational misalignment. The perfect time to examine your thoughts, feelings and beliefs in an effort to get to the core of why things are the way they are is when life is failing to bring you what you want.

The more you can recognize the mirror effect in your life, the more self-aware you will become. As others highlight your weaknesses, you can see what areas you might need to work on. If others show you disrespect, you need to look at how you disrespect yourself. If you find yourself surrounded by angry people, look at what you are angry with in yourself and your life. This works both ways – you are also a perfect mirror for others. If you show others love and honesty, you will find yourself surrounded by loving, honest people. Every day offers an opportunity to see what others are showing us and to work on our thoughts, beliefs and energy patterns.

Keep this in mind next time you have an argument with someone and have a look at the dynamics of on the situation. What is that person showing that you don't like within yourself? Everyone has things about themselves they would like to change. When we decide what we are going to do next in life, remember, that as we are stepping into change, what we believe about that change will be mirrored back to us. If we believe that the change we are making is perfect and it's going to make us happier, a positive experience will be mirrored back to us. However, if deep down we believe we can't make this change or we won't be good managing it, life will reflect that back to us.

The emotional scale

Esther and Jerry Hicks (*Ask and it is Given*) conceived of the emotional scale I'm sharing with you. As mentioned earlier we send vibrations or frequency into the universe. Our emotions influence the signal we send. The emotional scale indicates the level of vibration we are sending out into the universe. The emotions we want to create from are those at the top end of the scale such as joy, love and freedom. It is from these emotions that we can create what we want. Think about it....a simple example is that we can't create a happy family from a place of anger.

It's valuable to know what your emotional set point is - by this I mean the emotional level we return to and would consider our 'normal'. Throughout a single day we can experience a wide range of emotions. Our aim is to move the set point further up the scale to the positive emotions so our experiences mirror those emotions. The more we understand that each emotion has its own vibrational frequency and pattern, the easier it is to see how we help to create everything in our life. The emotional scale will give you a clear indication of whether there's work to do on your thoughts, feelings and beliefs. This is especially helpful when determining your next steps in life, as you want to make sure we feel good before taking any action.

The emotional scale basically consists of 22 levels of emotion. The highest level is joy, knowledge, empowerment, freedom, love and appreciation. Imagine that your decision about what you want to do next in your life fills you with joy as you approach the situation. If that is the case, you cannot help but be successful at whatever you chose to do. It is important to remember that your attitude toward your decision is as important as the decision itself, if not more so! When we live from those places of higher vibration, we experience the magic in life.

1. Joy, knowledge, empowerment, freedom, love, appreciation
2. Passion
3. Enthusiasm, eagerness, happiness
4. Positive expectation, belief
5. Optimism
6. Hopefulness
7. Content
8. Boredom
9. Pessimism
10. Frustration, irritation, impatience

11. Overwhelment
12. Disappointment
13. Doubt
14. Worry
15. Blame
16. Discouragement
17. Anger
18. Revenge
19. Hatred, rage
20. Jealousy
21. Insecurity, unworthiness
22. Fear, grief, despair, paralysis

We can use the emotional scale as a tool to determine where our vibration is at any moment in time. We can see what affects us and causes us to come crashing down emotionally. As we move up the scale, the goal is not to take giant leaps; it's to take baby steps. Normally we don't move from depression to joy, but we might move from depression to anger. Anger has a higher vibration than depression, so this movement is actually a step forward. If we are worried, we might ascend into pessimism, which is higher on the scale. As you start defining your dreams, note how they make you feel on that emotional scale. We can only create what we want from the higher vibrational states.

We may well decide that we want to do something specific, but if we feel really bad about it, or we are in a low vibrational state, the experience we create will not be good. This is important to understand as we make changes. This emotional scale has become one of my greatest tools helping me to understand my level of vibration at any time. Being aware that this scale exists and that we can make small shifts rather than take giant leaps, takes pressure off us: we don't have to succumb to all emotions, but we can recognize the emotion we are feeling and use it to clarify the direction we want to go.

We can also use the emotional scale as a guide when we do not feel good about a decision. As we are embarking on this new journey, we want to do so with a clear mind, a clear heart and with positive emotions to ensure that we experience success in our choice. Start to note the emotions you go through in a day and what they are telling you. Remember that conflict can occur when we try to think things through too much. However, if we follow our heart and use our emotions as a guide, we have a much better idea as to whether we are on the right track or we need to change.

Heartmath – Quick Coherence Technique™

Another terrific tool that I use is the Heartmath Quick Coherence™ technique. This is wonderful if you are stuck in one of those lower vibrational states. It was developed by the Heartmath Institute, in which scientists conduct research into heart functions and how we can create the different emotional states through our heart. I use this technique whenever I am conscious about wanting to shift up on the vibrational scale. For example, if I'm feeling worried I'll use the technique and it always shifts me immediately.

It's a very simple three-step process:

1. Focus your attention on the heart area around your chest. You might like to close your eyes, but you don't have to. I find it much easier when I do.

2. Breathe into your heart and take long slow breaths – in through your nose, out through your mouth. As you are breathing in, picture the air going in and filling that heart space in your chest.

3. Activate a feeling and bring that into your heart. When you are breathing in, you bring that feeling with your breath. The easiest way to do this is by finding a happy memory. One of the memories that I like to use is the first time that I ever stood up on a surfboard. I have only learnt to surf recently and I love the feeling I get when I am up and riding a wave. It's such a wonderful experience for me. It brings me joy and makes me feel connected to nature and more connected to myself. When I breathe that feeling into my heart I feel happier, more joyful and more excited about life. Find an experience or a picture that makes you

feel happy and just practice breathing it into your heart space. You will know you have found the right memory when doing this exercise moves you up the emotional scale.

Chapter Summary

Our heart has the most powerful energy field of the body and the ability to behave like a second brain. It is engaged in constant communication with, and can influence the head brain. Yet we inherently perceive the world by making sense of it with our head brain. If we only consider life in this context we are missing the opportunity to fully utilize our senses. When we make decisions from the heart, we will achieve better outcomes and feel happier when following our heart.

We use all parts of our brain to perform natural bodily functions. Our left and right hemispheres have specific functions that they are in charge of. We have the ability to utilize our whole brain through intention and using physical techniques such as the Cross Crawl March and the Lazy 8.

The more we try to make sense of our world, possibilities and our lives using only the head brain, the more we limit ourselves. Deep down, each of us knows the answer that is right for us. We do not need to seek confirmation from anyone else. We do need to take time to listen to what our heart is telling us. If you focus on the things that are most important to you, it will lead to a happier, more fulfilling life.

Everything that we see in our life is created through a mirror effect. This means that experiences are a reflection of our deepest thoughts and beliefs. Knowing this means we can look at the things we don't like in life and ask ourselves what it shows about us and what we might want to change.

The emotional scale is a valuable tool that ranks our emotions in terms of the positive power they have. We always want to create from higher-level emotions such as joy, love and freedom. This will ensure that we feel good along the way and create better outcomes and more of what we truly want. A great technique to move up the emotional scale is The Quick Coherence Technique™ that was developed by the Heartmath Institute.

Questions for self-reflection

1. Where on the emotional scale is my vibration located most of the time?

_____

_____

_____

_____

_____

2. What is one thing I can do to help raise this level?

_____

_____

_____

_____

_____

3. If I listen to my heart about what I truly want in life, what answer do I get?

_____

_____

_____

_____

_____

CHAPTER 6

FEELING CONNECTED

*There is a place of connection deep within each of us
and it is available at any time. When we engage with
ourselves at that deep spiritual level, we see how
amazing we truly are.*

When my children were very young we lived in Spain. In fact, my son was born therein. We decided to take the children for a holiday, and Paris was one of the cities we visited. Before we left people told me to make sure I held onto to my purse, and I had been advised not to use a backpack-style handbag. But that's what I had. One day we were travelling on the metro going to visit the Opera national de Paris. David had Lachlan, who was just a baby, and I had my daughter Rhian holding one hand and Morgan the other. To get to the platforms in the Metro we had to go down some steep escalators. As we were going down the escalators, I noticed a group of three young girls behind me but didn't think anything of it. I was busily monitoring my two children, making sure they were getting on and off the escalator safely.

When we arrived at the opera house, I went to buy something and discovered that my handbag was undone and, sure enough, my purse was missing. Of course I had just been to an ATM, so I had lots of cash in there ready for our holiday. I knew that it was the young girls who had taken the wallet out of my bag. I didn't get angry, but I was quite disappointed at the time because I had some cards in my wallet that were special to me. There was nothing we could do about it; there was no one to report it to, so we continued with our holiday and I started looking for a new handbag!

I remember saying to the universe, "I know the cash is gone, but please bring my purse back to me because I want those cards." If you are familiar with the Paris Metro you know that people do not get their stolen wallets back. My friends in Spain told me to forget about it, renew all the cards and move on. I was hanging on to this idea that I was going to get my purse back and didn't care what others told me. A couple of weeks later David took me out purse shopping. I wasn't really interested in finding a new purse because I had fixated on getting my old one returned to me. David and my friends all thought I was crazy, but somewhere inside of me I had absolute faith that I would get it back.

Three weeks later, I received a letter from the Paris Metro station where my purse had been taken, saying they had found my purse. All the cards were inside but there was no cash, and if I would like it back I could just send 16 Euro to them and they would post it to me. I sent the 16 Euro, got my purse back and indeed, all my cards were there. What was so striking for me about the experience was my absolute faith in getting them back, not the fact that I got the purse or the cards. I believed so strongly that the universe was bringing my purse back to me and I didn't listen to what anyone said. I also let go of whether or not it would come back – I would have been happy either way.

Although this might seem unrelated to rediscovering who we are, this story shows how powerful our intention and beliefs can be. It taught me that when we listen to our intuition, we have an inexplicable sense of knowing. It is wonderful for us to develop this faith and belief in the universe but to do so we need to feel connected to our self/highest spirit/source/inner knowing – whatever you prefer to call it.

In this chapter I discuss concepts around feeling connected. At the end of the chapter I will give you a few exercises to practice tuning in and starting to listen to the side of you that knows about the magic in this world.

Do you accept that you are amazing?

When asking mothers about their children, I find it astonishing that they can always see how amazing their children are and how they have the potential to do anything. Similarly, they can look at other mothers and see the amazing job that mothers do. Very rarely, though, can they look at themselves with those same eyes; instead, they become critical and judgmental of themselves. It is much easier to find other people inspiring.

I am not talking about seeing our self in an egotistical manner; rather, I am referring to the gentle inner knowledge that we appreciate and value who we are and what we bring to the world. If we can perceive others as amazing, we must find a way to look at ourselves through those same eyes. When we do, we feel better; we can be open to more possibilities, and we are willing to try anything. We will make decisions from a different point of view because we can believe that we too are amazing. In many ways, we have all held ourselves back, but the ability to see ourselves as extraordinary human beings begins to change the way we relate to the world and the world to us.

When do I judge myself?

Most people are constantly judging the way they look, the way they keep house, the way their children behave, whether they are good enough and on and on. We tend to focus on our flaws rather than the things that we like about ourselves. Yet when we ask other people what they see in us, they will have a very different vision of who we are. They don't hold those same harsh judgments.

The only cure for judgment is acceptance! When we move into a place of self-acceptance, acceptance of other people and situations as just being what they are, rather than being good or bad, our outlook on life changes. I am actively practicing acceptance, and as a consequence, I feel much happier in all aspects of my life. Of course, I still want to create change at a personal level, but right now I accept who I am and I can love myself. It is easy to see beauty in everyone when listening carefully to your source/spirit. Our source has all the answers we need but often we don't listen – if we did, many of our life decisions would be very different. Listening to our inner self is similar to listening to our heart, because it is where our ultimate self-knowledge originates, where we are not over-thinking whether our decision will lead us down the "right" road.

When we relate this to what we want to do next it's the same thing …we need to listen to our source. At a deep, unconscious level, we already know what to do next. We know what we want, where we want to go and the best next step for us. It is just that most of us don't listen. Listening to your source does not mean that you have to meditate for hours every day, though you may like to do this. It is more about listening and allowing some quiet time for reflection and to listen in the moment when it is time to make a decision. We tend to do this instinctively as mothers – we know what we are supposed to do when our children get sick, when they're hurt or when they need us for something. We don't tend to use this same instinct as much when determining our next step or ponder our possibilities. I invite you to take some time to sit in quiet reflection or find a way for you to best listen to your source. You might like to try one of the tools provided at the end of this chapter.

There is no point tuning in and asking for answers if you are not going to listen to them. Remember, sometimes those answers will not make sense to your head brain, but if they make sense to your heart, then they provide the path to follow. That is the path that ultimately will bring you more happiness. In today's society, there are plenty of people telling us what we should be doing and what's best for us, but in the end only you know exactly what is right for you. There are people who we will learn from, who have skills, knowledge and experience and who are where we want to be. Listen to those people, but if they say something that conflicts with what you know to be true in your heart for you, then you need to consider that and listen to yourself.

What is universal consciousness?

Although this topic alone could fill a book, I mention it here because it helps to understand the context of "me" in a bigger picture. When we understand the principle of universal consciousness, we know that everything we do, think and say has a far greater effect than just on our own life. It contributes universal consciousness even though we are just one very small piece of the matrix. I call it a matrix because I imagine universal consciousness like a massive net or web that connects everything.

We all have our unique perspectives, but when enough people are thinking in the same way, it raises universal consciousness to a new level. The example that is often used is the four-minute mile barrier. For years, man believed that it was not possible to run a mile in under four minutes; however, Rodger Bannister disagreed. History shows that once he broke that barrier, in a very short period of time, others started also to break it: Bannister had broken through the collective consciousness. History is littered with examples that show clearly how a consciousness barrier was broken. The more we raise the overall vibration of consciousness, the more different the world will be. Basically, every one of your thoughts travels into this web or ether, and that thought helps to create a collective consciousness.

There is a collective consciousness around the financial state of the world. In the past I heard myself say to my children, "We can't afford that." Of course, that was the experience I created, but it also added to the consciousness of lack in our world, when in reality, there is abundance for everyone. Whatever you are thinking is contributing to something that is greater than you. There is so little in our world we can see, but we can feel the truth of the existence of energy and somehow, deep inside, we know that a universal consciousness exists. As more of us are able to develop into the person we want to be, the more we can break down barriers and resistance and the more others will be able to do the same.

The power of love

I have talked about the emotional scale where love is one of the highest vibrational forces in the universe. Any situation you choose to look at from a perspective of love will change. You gain greater clarity about people and how things in your life came into being. When your decisions come from a place of love, everything will feel easier, lighter; you will feel more in alignment with yourself and who you want to be. In my experience, we also feel more peace when we simply love; when we have no resistance to how extraordinary human beings are and how incredible we are all together in this beautiful world. I mention this because it is vitally important that the path you want to choose and what you want your life to look like comes from a place of love. Most mothers find it easy to look at their children from a place of love and to understand how important love is in their life. We see it daily –

when our children feel loved, they respond differently, behave better and they appear more confident. They can face challenges and they perform better in their journey of learning. The same applies to you as you explore who you are. Think about how much you love yourself and whether you recognize your value. This book is about recognizing who you are, that you have value, and that you can be or do whatever you want.

What really jazzes me?

Those things that make us feel happiest are a good indication of what we want to be doing. Know what brings you the most joy in life and what makes your heart sing. For many, it's about helping other people, but that help can come in many different forms. Some people love to go into a school and read with children, others want to go and work in a home for the elderly to keep them company, while for others it's just listening to people and helping them overcome a problem. Whether or not it is about helping others, the most important thing is to become clear about what makes you feel really happy and identify what you want to bring more of into your life. With such clarity, you can begin to get a sense of the direction that is right for you. Before I had babies, I had a clear vision of who I was, but when I became a mother that vision changed dramatically. When my children went off to school, this changed again and, of course, going through a separation and divorce, that picture changed yet again. During each of these times, I underwent a transformation.

As we realize that we are in a transformational stage, there is no rush to get anywhere or be anything different from what we are. This realization is simply that, at this point in time, we are contemplating whether or not we want to continue being the same person we have been or whether it is time to change. Your answer doesn't matter, but your awareness of choice does. You always have a choice about whether or not you want to transform and about whether the choices you are making are based upon love or fear. For many years I chose to hold myself back, not because anyone told me to do so, but because deep down I didn't know how – I didn't see how I could be a mother and run a business at the same time, so I chose primarily to be a mother for my children.

Now I know that my beliefs were limiting my vision, and I find my children are growing with me every day. We are moving into such an exciting period of life, and I watch them as they see possibilities open for themselves as a result of me stepping into a bigger vision for all of us.

Who do I want to be?

This is the ultimate question to consider. We all have a perception of who we are and who we were in the past, but not necessarily of whom we are going to be in the future. Now is the time to make a conscious choice. For the last few years, you've probably focused upon being a mother, which normally means being a cook, cleaner, diaper changer, washer, nurse, etc. Ultimately, we all want to be the best mothers that we can, and we want our children to have a good experience of life. As our children are now at school, we have an opportunity to consider who we want to be other than a mother. Again, what we actually choose doesn't matter so much, as long as we feel good about our choice. We can be playful about our choices because we can always change them later. Don't be paralyzed by the thought that what you choose now must be forever. We can always re-invent our self at any point in time throughout our life. The essential "me" will be fairly consistent if you listen to your heart, but the way you express yourself to the world might be different.

As we develop our goals and hold a vision for ourselves, we need to consider who we want to be along the journey. Life is not about reaching a particular destination; it's about the journey and the person we become along the way. Whatever decisions you want to make about your future, think about what you want to look like, how you carry yourself, what you think about, what you read, the way you dress etc. That will help to build a picture of who you want to be and what you want to do. Keep in mind that you can be and do whatever you decide. The only thing that stops us from being or doing what we want is us, and when we can get clear about that we are free to choose anything.

Developing intuition

We all have natural intuition, and it is available to all of us free of charge. The point is whether we actually practice connecting to this intuition and whether we listen to it. If you are unsure of how to tune into your intuition, rest assured that you can learn. The more we connect to our intuition, the more finely tuned we become. Now messages come quickly to me and I trust those messages implicitly. The guidance is almost always clear from my intuition. I say "almost" because there are certain emotional states that totally block intuition when I fall into them. They are always lower vibrational states such as anger or guilt. The more conscious we can become at tuning in at those times, the more quickly we will raise our vibration. For instance, if one of my children misbehaves, it is not because they are naughty; rather, it is because something emotional is going on for them. Sometimes I respond to the behavior and then stop and realize there's something more going on for my child. That is when I can tune into my intuition and ask what they need right now.

When making decisions about life, our intuition will lead us in the right direction, provided we listen. If that has not been a part of your life, you're not alone! For some of you it will feel natural and for others it's not going to come as easily. Most people already use intuition somewhere in their lives, particularly as mothers when we look after our children and their needs. It's a matter of learning how to use intuition more in our everyday life. Doing so gradually reduces the time, energy and effort you need because you will know immediately what action to take. Playing with your intuition is lots of fun and you can develop it quickly and easily with the right intention.

Ways we intuit information?

There are four main ways that intuitive information comes to people. There are others as well, but those presented below resonate for most people. Notice if one of the following feels right for you:

Clairaudient (Hearing) People for whom this ability is well developed will hear messages; they might hear sounds, words, full messages or scattered words. Innately they will interpret the sounds and know what they mean. In the dark ages when people heard voices they were considered crazy or to be witches. Is it possible that they were hearing intuitive messages? If you hear whispers every now and again that you can't place, stop and take note, because maybe for you intuition comes in a clairaudient fashion.

Clairvoyant (Visual) Some people might see words, but more than likely they will see a vision of something that occurs in the future or something that is happening now. It may be in the form of a movie or still photographs. This kind of intuition can show you which direction you are supposed to take because you see it very clearly.

Clairsentient (Feeling) People who are clairsentient have a feeling that they should do something a particular way or go somewhere. People who intuit this way just have a feeling, sometimes like emotional guidance, but normally a reaction in the Solar Plexus area. The saying "A knot in our stomach" reflects the experience of a clairsentient intuitive.

Claircognizant (Knowing) Claircognizant people simply know the answer or direction. I intuit like this, and I can't explain how I know things. It's like I am reaching up to a source that is greater than myself, pulling back this information and bringing it into my mind. When I am with clients I will often receive information this way that I then convey to them. It's always fun when they look at me in amazement.

You will have had experiences throughout your life in which you relied on your intuition. For some, their intuition was blocked in childhood, so they may have to go far back to remember. If one of the above four ways of intuiting information jumps out at you more than the others, go with it. It's a matter of practicing and listening to the way that you intuit information. If you are still unsure, play with each of them. Use the exercises at the end of this chapter to learn which way you intuit best.

Can I trust my intuition?

The hardest part of listening to your intuition is to trust the messages you receive. There is no point learning to listen if you are not prepared to trust and follow the messages. People get caught up trying to make logical sense of their intuition, which only creates confusion. This comes back to us through trying to control the way things will happen in our lives. For example, I might get a message to go to a particular shop. I don't know why I am being guided there; I just know I need to go there and when I get there I will know more. We won't always see the whole picture - we may just get the next step. The more comfortable we can be following our guidance without knowing the full picture, the easier we will find it to trust, and the better it will feel. When you realize that everything in your life happens for your highest good, you know that you can trust your intuition. Even the incidence about my purse being stolen in Paris was, I know, absolutely for my highest good because it opened my trust in listening to my own intuition. That very situation taught me to trust the messages I am receiving.

When we listen to our intuition on some of the big issues in life, it can be a little more daunting to trust what we are getting because of the perceived consequences. For many mothers, even deciding whether to go to work can feel overwhelming, but in reality they are simply forgetting that they can always change their mind. When you can tune into your intuition about the right next step for you and then trust it, you begin to move with more confidence that you are following your path. But when you doubt your intuition, it will affect the experiences you are creating; instead, your experiences will match your doubt. They will "prove" you were right to be doubtful.

There are times when intuition will download and your brain will understand perfectly why you need to take a particular action. When you are beginning to learn to use your intuition, start with some of the smaller things in your life – the little things that aren't going to matter even if you feel you like you got them wrong. Developing your intuition to a point where you just trust it might take a bit of work and effort, but it is 100 % worth it.

Exercises to develop intuition.

Daily play – This is one of my favorite ways to begin expanding intuition and trusting it. Daily play is about having fun with your intuition and using it in a non-threatening way. Before your phone rings guess who's calling (without looking at the caller ID); before you open your e-mails guess how many e-mails are in your inbox. Guess who's at your door, how many letters you will get, or anything else you want! It's about having fun with it and not getting caught up whether you are right or wrong. What matters more is that you are learning to integrate the habit of listening to your intuition. Let go of needing to be right and just be playful.

Suspend one sense – This is another of my favorite games that I often play with my children. Our intuition goes well beyond our knowledge, awareness, experience and our other senses. We process the world through the five main senses – sight, sound, smell, taste, and touch. When we suspend one of our five main senses, our other senses become more sensitive. For instance, close your eyes and you will notice more sounds than you did when you had your eyes open. If you block off your sense of smell while you are cooking, the cooking experience is less pleasurable. If you block off your ears, you will see things differently. Try suspending one of your senses and notice which other sense increases in activation. This is a fun way to become more aware of our senses.

Partnering – Partnering is another exercise that I love, but when I first tried it I found it daunting. For this exercise you need a friend, preferably someone who is also interested in developing his or her intuition. Make sure it's someone with whom you feel very safe. Ask them to give you the name and age of a person that they know (who you don't know) and then sit quietly and tune in to any information you receive about that person and share it with your partner. You will notice doubt will creep in when you try this exercise. It's important that you move past the doubt and become light and playful with it. Share whatever information comes immediately to your mind and allow the other person to reflect back whether or not it's correct. Do not take it so seriously that it inhibits you. Have fun with it and allow it to develop your intuition. You may also find that the relationship you have with the partner will deepen as you both feel safe exploring.

Chapter Summary

In order to achieve a connection to our source/higher self/spirit/universe we need to see and feel that we are part of a bigger picture. Within that picture, all humans are amazing, including you! Every time we judge our self as being good or bad, we remain stuck. Only by accepting who you are now can you bring in any change. Judgment is a terrible affliction that can leave us feeling miserable.

Universal consciousness is a collective "agreement" that we all have decided to believe. For instance, for many years everyone believed the world was flat. Now we know that is not true, and it is difficult to imagine that people once believed this. I wonder what humanity will look back upon in 200 years and feel the same way about. Every thought we have contributes to universal consciousness, so the more we explore the truth about our self, the more we contribute to the evolution of human consciousness.

Love is the most powerful force in the universe. It really needs to be the basis for all of our thoughts, actions and decisions. We may see some success coming from other perspectives, but we will succeed if our intentions stem from love. Whatever you want to choose next, make sure it's something you love.

As you are considering your future life, think about what excites you. We can formulate many reasons for why we can't have, be or do something – in the end that's just an expression of our self as well. If we do the work and define in detail who we want to be, we are more likely to grow into that person. Every time we are faced with a decision we have the choice to be more or less like the person we want to be.

It is exciting to begin using your intuition for more of your decision-making. When you first begin it can be frightening to trust the messages you receive, especially if they don't make sense to your logical brain. The more you practice "tuning in", the more you will learn to trust those messages.

We intuit information in four main ways: Clairaudient (hearing), Clairvoyant (seeing), Clairsentient (feeling), Claircognizant (knowing). No one way is better than the other and everyone is different. The most important aspect, no matter how you intuit, is to trust what you are receiving. If you have doubt you will create more of those circumstances!

Three exercises that are wonderful for developing the intuition are: Daily Play, Suspend one sense and Partnering. Your intuition will develop if you play with these. Let go of needing any outcome to be "right" and enjoy the process of learning.

Questions for self-reflection

1. In what areas do I judge myself to be not good enough? How does this affect my feelings about myself?

_____

_____

_____

_____

_____

2. Who is it that I want to become – define what I want to look like, dress like, my posture, behavior, friends, thoughts.

_____

_____

_____

_____

_____

3. What exercise will I incorporate into my life to develop my intuition?

_____

_____

_____

_____

_____

CHAPTER 7

YOU HAVE UNIQUE GIFTS AND TALENTS

Each of us brings gifts and talents to the world, whether or not we recognize them. It takes courage to show our talents with an open heart and mind without falling into the ego trap.

One of the most difficult concepts I've learned to grasp has been to acknowledge that I have unique gifts and talents. In the past I thought academic success was an important measurement of success. As I grow older I realize that most of my knowledge and skills have come from pursuing avenues of learning that most interest me through courses, reading, listening to others and learning through my experiences. One of my gifts is the fun-loving perspective I have on life. I also have an ability to make people feel good about who they are while motivating them to create the change they want. It has taken me a long time to accept these gifts. The neural pathways I had developed kept me focusing on what I hadn't achieved or studied. I can now acknowledge that I chose a path that suited me; even though it differs from the path many others choose. Although it has taken time to see my gifts and talents I now appreciate them immensely.

As you read through this chapter contemplate how you feel about your gifts and talents. Many people will have quite some resistance to the idea they have talent, or they will only acknowledge what they perceive to be small things. Sadly, many people never realize how much each of us does bring into the world.

Breaking down internal resistance ...

Everyone brings different gifts and talents to the world. There's no one on this earth who has the same perspective, skills and experiences as you do. When I became a mother, I felt that my work-based skills were put to the side because my focus was on being a mother. When I talk to other women, I hear the same; they want to focus on motherhood and give their kids the best possible opportunities, so they give up paid employment. After a few years, their skills may have dissipated, become outdated or worse, they may have lost their self-confidence.

If we fail to acknowledge and accept our gifts and talents, we do a disservice to our children as well as to ourselves. People learn best by example, so if we want our children to recognize that they have innate skills, abilities and talents, we must acknowledge ours. We are the role models showing them how to accept that they are amazing and that they have gifts.

We need people doing all sorts of things in the world. It would be a boring world if everyone had the same skills and talents! We need people who can make others smile, work in a bank, drive a rubbish truck and those who feel comfortable speaking to thousands. Whatever you choose, it only matters that you are bringing your spirit into your everyday life with integrity and that you are allowing yourself to shine.

When is the last time that you acknowledged your talents?

You decide what you want to share with the world. No one else can decide that for you. If you have a message that you want to express, whether through words, art, being a mother or some other form, find the way that feels good to you. I love it when people ask me about my children, what they are doing and what they are good at, because I am so enthusiastic when I describe how amazing they are. My children play music and sports, they have fun and they enjoy technology. I watch them and see they can do anything they decide they want. It's very easy to tell other people how amazing my children are, and I hear other mothers say the same. I love to see a mother's eyes light up when she talks about her child/children.

On the whole, mothers are proud of their children and can see their strengths in the form of talents and weaknesses that they need to develop. When we reflect upon ourselves, we find it much harder to determine our talents and skills or to even accept that we have any. We live in an era in which we should be wise enough to apply those same eyes to ourselves – to see and acknowledge that we have skills and talents. It is time for each of us to own our greatness and stop hiding behind false perceptions.

How can I juggle everything?

Motherhood is a constant juggle trying to fit everything in and find some balance. We have 24 hours in a day and we can only fit so much into that time. If you watch a juggler they start with 3 balls and continue to add more. Normally they can manage to keep 6-8 balls consistently in the air. But add or miss one ball and they all fall down. This is a little like us – we continue to add to what we juggle as mothers and at some point either collapse or drop things that are important to us. I have found it easier to be clear about my priorities and focus on them during each 24-hour period. When my children were babies, there was no balance. All my energy was dedicated to making sure they had what that they needed. I was blessed to be able to play golf every now and again or have coffee with friends, but my life wasn't balanced. Contrary to many theories and beliefs, I have found that, as I let go of seeking balance, focusing on doing the things that bring me joy instead, I am happier and healthier.

If you have goals and dreams, your life may well seem out of balance as you work towards those goals. You will have to put some effort into changing your life, give up some things and take focused action. Society has us believe that we must be balanced, however this can keep us chasing an elusive dream really only available to those with excessive income. When you are doing what you truly love, balance becomes less important because you are already happy.

Chapter 9 is dedicated solely to this subject; it will give you ideas about how you can manage your priorities. What is most important is that your focus is on what you want out of life and that you take some action every day toward where you want to go rather than succumbing to your routines. People who are following their dreams don't have balance in their lives. They are dedicated, focused and know what they want. To us, this doesn't mean putting our children on the sidelines while we follow our dreams. Children are most mothers' main priority. Each of us has to work out what feels right in terms of motherhood, our dreams and the life we truly want.

As I strive toward my goals I find my children developing and growing with me. They are learning to be more independent and take more responsibility for the things they want. My dream includes my children - I share my vision with them so they have some understanding and want to see these dreams come true as well.

My children now have their own vision boards, dreams and goals. I have a 13-year-old who is writing her own book as well as her own music. My 11-year-old is a videographer for a local business and she is creating all sorts of amazing things using modern technology. They all play sport and music and enjoy being with friends. It's so exciting to see them expand their possibilities. I am no longer seeking "balance" and would rather take actions to follow my dreams.

What does life purpose mean to me?

While we can look up the definition of purpose in a dictionary, the meaning of life's purpose differs between people. What it meant to us when we were young might be quite different now that we have become mothers. Let's explore two ways of looking at life purpose – perhaps one will resonate more strongly with you than the other. The idea of this discussion is to open your mind to new ways of thinking, not to sway you one way or the other. Choose what feels right to you. Your thoughts of purpose will be affected by the way you see life in general.

1. *Life Purpose as a destiny:* many people spend years searching, seeking to discover their life purpose. They ask questions such as "Who am I?", "Why am I here?", "What am I here to do?" I have found particularly in our

30s and 40s women start to explore these questions. There's a knowingness inside that there is more to life than we have realised so far.

2. *Life Purpose as a choice:* rather than seeking our purpose, this idea enables us to decide what our purpose is and who we want to become. This empowers us to choose what feels good and to change our minds at times.

Although many of us can understand elements of both viewpoints, they can also leave us feeling an internal conflict. Are we deciding or discovering our purpose? I'll share my experience of these views and let you make up your mind.

For many years I was searching for something more; I was sure I had some purpose to fulfill in the world but I couldn't work out what it was. I over-thought it and found the answer wouldn't come to me no matter whether I meditated on it, undertook energy healing, read books or attended seminars. I would look for signs from the universe, little messages that could help guide me in the right direction. What I found was that focusing solely on this way of thinking kept me paralyzed from taking action, for I wanted to make sure I was following the "right" path. More recently, I've decided to choose the path I want to follow in life.

I ask myself questions such as:

- What if my purpose were to explore this playground we call Earth?
- What if my purpose were simply to be happy?
- What if, by taking action, my purpose will become clearer to me?
- What if there is no destined purpose and it was all choice?
- What if my life passed by and I never made the choice?

Once I made some decisions, I felt empowered and inspired. When making these decisions I listened to my heart and did what felt good. Doing this has moved me out of paralysis and expanded my thinking around purpose. I don't know if there is one destined purpose for each of us; I only know that I feel happier, more fulfilled and energized by what I do. Perhaps this is in alignment with a destined purpose and perhaps not.

The beautiful thing about life is that we can all choose our viewpoint. If you choose to be a mother at this point in your life, then enjoy it without questioning if you need to be doing anything else. If you feel something inside pulling at you, explore it. Focus more on being happy each day in what you are doing while articulating or working towards your dreams. Take time to consider what purpose means to you, whether it has changed over time and whether you are holding yourself back from a bigger view.

Regardless of whether you see purpose as a destiny or choice, if you have some unfulfilled dreams, there will be actions you can take now to move toward those dreams. As you take one action, other steps will become clearer to you. I liken it to pieces of a big jigsaw puzzle. At some point you will see some consistency in your life, and see how your experiences, knowledge and skills tie together. But when you are paralyzed and standing still, you are stagnating and your dreams remain out of reach.

How do I balance my needs with my family's needs?

Most mothers want to be mothers, which means we think about our family and children when making decisions. Everything we do is role modeling for our children, including the way we see the world and the possibilities we see for ourselves. If we are fearful of expressing ourselves creatively or of following our passions, we are teaching our children this. I want to instill in my children that mothers can be loving, energetic and vibrant and still work toward their dreams.

Everyone will have different dreams; only you can decide what the right vision looks and feels like for you. It is no one else's business but yours what that vision is. Do not let the judgments of others affect what your heart truly desires. When our children head off to school, it's a great time to evaluate your direction in life. The decisions you choose today have an impact on your future life.

I only recently began truly to understand that the choices I made in the moment affected both my enjoyment of the present moment and the future I was creating. If I was choosing to be unhappy in the moment, I was not only creating discord in the moment but it had a longer term affect in what I believed was possible. This is why I say to use emotions as a guidance system, rather than a decision-making system. If you are feeling angry, it shows that something in your life is not the way you want it to be. Instead of making a decision from a place of anger, notice the anger and allow it to show you what you don't want. Then when you've calmed down, listen to your heart for the right next step. Once you have made a decision, commit to it. Break through any barriers of fear, anxiety or doubt and know that you can do it if you stay focused. If the decision comes from your heart and is in alignment with what you want out of life do not allow anyone to sway you. You will find the way to balance the needs of your family with your own … if you commit to it.

I used to think that I had to be available to play with my children whenever they wanted. When they were younger I'd spend hours playing with them, but as they grow older they are able to amuse themselves. Instead of feeling guilty that I'm not always available, I make sure that when we are together and playing we are fully engaged and having a great time. One of their favorite games is spotlight in the house. We turn off all the lights at night and play hide and seek with a flashlight. We are constantly laughing and squealing in delight as we play. I realized that what I wanted was for my children to feel loved and adored, as well as to spend time with them while they're growing up. That didn't mean I needed to be available all the time, however. The old beliefs I had about my family's needs were part of what caused me to hold back for so long.

I have forgotten everything I used to know!

Before I had children, I worked in the corporate world. I was savvy, remembered everything and was very good at my job. After I had been at home for a few years with the children, I wondered if I still had those abilities. The problem is not so much that we forget what it was like to work or the skills we used, but because we lose our confidence. When we begin to think of reentering the workforce we start to wonder what can we do now. I have met so many amazing women with incredible skills, yet their confidence level has dropped so much. A lot of these women don't want to go back to work the way it was before children, so they lower their expectations of what is possible in a job for them.

Our value as a person with talents and skills does not diminish because we choose to be at home with our children. In fact, we learn a great deal of different life skills during this period of our life. If you have forgotten things that you used to know you can re-learn them. If you want to do something new, you can learn that too. You have a great deal of knowledge already – don't underestimate it! It doesn't matter that we have forgotten some things. What is more important is that we don't limit our vision because we fear not having the skills to do what we really want to do.

If you are considering getting a job, think about what work you would like to be doing, rather than what you perceive as possible. Imagine the type of work, the hours, company and the people you'd like to work with, how you would feel and how your day would look. We don't have to put limitations on ourselves if we are willing to work and learn. Confidence comes from within us; it is not about what we remember from before we had our children. It is more about what we are willing to learn, the effort we are prepared to put into life and what we believe we can have out of life. Confidence is about how you feel about yourself. Most confidence issues come from our thoughts, from a place of judgment that we are not doing enough or that we are not good enough. We could all change this if we saw ourselves from that same loving perspective from which we look at our children.

You don't need to know all the skills right now and you don't need to let your past limit who you want to be in the future. But you do have to know who you want to be, and feel confident that you are capable of being, or becoming, that person. If you are feeling trapped because you must go back to work for financial reasons, find a job and do whatever it is you feel you need to do at this point, but keep clarifying your future vision. Know with your heart and your head that you can learn whatever skills and knowledge you need to move toward whatever it is you want.

How do I identify my unique skills and talents?

The first step is to accept and acknowledge that you have some skills and talents. Even though this sounds basic, it is vital to recognize our strengths. To deny we have any will keep us feeling small and untalented. When we underestimate and undervalue ourselves (and others), we will relate to people in a way that doesn't allow our brilliance to show. We have comfort zones about our existence and the possibilities life has for us. We live in a perfect time to challenge those comfort zones and beliefs we have created.

To identify your unique talents and strengths ask your friends what they love about you and what they see in you. You might like to undertake a personal strengths and weaknesses analysis. This is where you write down your strengths – anything from personality traits, skills, abilities, etc. Then identify and write down your weaknesses. Inevitably, when I have done this exercise with people they find it very easy to identify the weaknesses and much harder to admit their strengths. As you identify these, focus on being supportive. This exercise is to give you some clarity about where you are now and to know whether you need to develop some new skills. When you start to see your strengths, weaknesses, skills, knowledge and experiences as unique you start to gain more confidence. What I can promise you is that you are unique!

When I was a child, I loved to play sport (almost any sport). I could play 24 hours a day and be perfectly happy! I still love sport and even though I am not partaking in it as much at this point of my life, when I do I am happy to be physically moving my body and being competitive. I know that, as an alternative career, anything to do with sport would have made me very happy. It was always a passion of mine and it has continued through my life. We all have some things that we did as children that we loved or things we would have really liked to do. Identifying those things that we loved as a child and were passionate about can be a good indicator as to what direction you would enjoy. Think back to when you were a child to what it was that brought you joy and have a look if there are some clues to your uniqueness.

What inspires me?

Many people just follow along the drudgery of life and don't think about being inspired or motivated. Now we share a quote on Facebook and we think that is where we get our inspiration. We are supposed to live with inspiration every day. Emotional motivation and support helps us on our journey, because, when we feel inspired, we want to engage in life more fully. We can step out of our present life view and feel more motivated to create what we want in our future. This is not about being in action all the time! This is about developing a mindset that will support you as you make changes. It is more important to be clear mentally, spiritually and emotionally and to have supportive thoughts patterns than it is to take action everyday. That's why I say if the only thing you do is to work on feeling good your life will transform. This is hard to understand because we are so used to controlling things in our life or thinking we have control over everything. Listening to people who are where we want to be will help us grow and develop as well as inspire us.

When we are in an inspired space we are in a better place to listen to our intuition and to follow the guidance that we receive. We will know what the next step is for us rather than taking action every day and feeling like we are constantly in motion without going anywhere. Find those people who inspire you and listen to what they say. When I a watch YouTube video or listen to an audio, nothing inspires me more than listening to the story of someone, especially of how they have overcome or built up their life and how they have stayed motivated. When you see that "ordinary" people can make good from almost anything in their life, you begin to understand the power that we all have. If you can find that inspiration every day it can help you feel good and stay motivated. The more inspired you feel the more it will help to prepare you for the future that you want.

Mindset, mindset, mindset!

If you can take responsibility for any limitations you decided to put on yourself, you can also choose to let go of them. While others may have contributed to the thinking that created the mindset, it was you who chose to continue that thinking. At any point in time you have the ability to choose how you think about yourself, your life, your past, present and your future. You can choose to think strongly or weakly. To develop a strong mindset you will need to work at it for you are not used to maintaining a positive attitude all the time. When we focus on people's weaknesses or compare ourselves to others it is damaging for our psyche. This is why staying inspired is so important because you need to keep nurturing your mindset. Mindset is simply a pattern about the way you choose to think. You can choose that now is the perfect time to make decisions and changes or you can choose that it will be later in your life – neither is right or wrong. But if your mindset isn't strong and you are not focused with purpose, you will keep wandering around not being sure of what's right for you.

It is vital that we develop a strong mindset, stay inspired every day and that we surround ourselves with people who will support us rather than bringing us down. You will have some thinking patterns and habits that do not support you. Developing mindset is about mental toughness, being conscious of your thoughts and changing them when you know they are not serving you. You have to be very strong, to have no doubts so that when people say you can't do something, you know otherwise. We can be susceptible to the doubt of others very quickly.

Find the vision that works for you and include your family in it. If you don't know exactly how that looks that's okay, but remember in your mind you can decide whether or not your family will fit in your picture. If your mindset is that you can't be fulfilled working and still be a good mother you will create that experience. If you are willing to open up and allow the universe to help you, and you maintain a strong mindset you will achieve what you want to.

Shifting out of my comfort zone

"Comfort zone" is a very interesting concept because it doesn't necessarily mean that you are comfortable there; it just means you know that place well. To some people, a comfort zone may only mean that they have enough money just to pay the bills. Even though they may not like that place and it's not comfortable there, they understand it well so it becomes their comfort zone. They don't know, and oftentimes cannot even imagine, what would be like to have an excess of money so they could choose to do whatever they want.

Living within their comfort zone prevents people from living their dream. They don't have to explore what they want out of life or where they are going because they are stuck in this zone. All of us have comfort zones related to our friends, how we fit in our family, how we are parents, how much money we have, what we look like on the outside and inside. To move out of our comfort zone means taking risks, trying new things and creating change. Lots of people don't like change because it moves them out of their comfort zone. It can be frightening to open up to new possibilities in life. When I reflect back on my life and where I am now, I wonder what happened and what I did in those years before I was following my passion. I know that moving out of my comfort zone is moving me toward my dreams far quicker than I could imagine. Maybe you don't want to change, and if you are happy with your life right now and everything feels perfect, that's great. But if there is that little voice that says, "I think there is something more I'd like," whether its big or small, then start listening to what your intuition is saying. Start doing some of the things I talk about in this book and answer the questions. Make sure that where you are going is where you want to go. Make sure that you are not sitting in your comfort zone because that's what you expect out of life.

You will not grow or move toward your dreams unless you change things. To create a life different from the one you are now living, you must get out of your comfort zone. There are no exceptions to this. Just remember that the comfort zone can be whatever you decide and this is why mindset is so important. As we focus on where we want to go, it's okay if it feels uncomfortable. I don't believe that you are reading this book by accident – there is something more that you want out of life, whether it's feeling happy about the life you have chosen, pursuing a career or artistic talent, new relationships or you want your body to look and feel differently. There is generally something that we want and this is the way life is supposed to be, because if we are stagnant, we are not growing.

Even the most successful people in the world, and by success I don't mean only financial, always have a goal they want to achieve. They have purpose and are passionate about what they do. They have a clear vision about themselves, they take action and they are constantly moving out of their comfort zone. Understand that you have a comfort zone that you have been in for a long time. A comfort zone feels like it gets smaller when we become a mother because we have little people in our life to think about and worry about. Challenge yourself regarding your comfort zone. Remember what it was like when you were younger before you had children and think about what's it like now...there may some things you need to change in your mindset to move out of the comfort zone that you have created.

Chapter Summary

Everyone has unique gifts and talents, but we tend to fail to recognize these in ourselves. We are self-critical and focus either on a path of self-improvement or one of unawareness. When we choose to hide and not show our talents we role model that for our children. Remembering to share our gifts and talents with the world means we need to do so from a heart space, not a place of ego.

Sometimes we find it easier to manage all our motherly actions; this keeps us from fully expressing our gifts. It is a full-time job just to live! You can only do so much in a 24-hour period. Unless you can change your thinking and start prioritizing time for you and your dreams, including how you might show your uniqueness, you will remain stuck in a routine.

Life's purpose can be viewed either as a destiny or a decision. Those who look at it from the destiny perspective can spend years searching for their true purpose, seeking clues from the universe or their inner being. Those who decide what they want from life generally are focused and move into action to see where each journey will lead. There may or may not be a destiny for each of us, however unless we make some decisions about what we want out of life, this way of thinking can be paralyzing.

Only you know how important family is to you. Rather than limiting what you think is possible, expand your vision to include your family. Whatever you believe about making time for yourself and your dreams, you will see it spring to life. If you feel guilty about going to work, you will create situations bringing more of that feeling, particularly when you are working. If you feel you can only find a job that you don't enjoy because that's all that's available during school hours, you will find a job that feels that way. You don't have to know how anything will work out, you just need to have a clear vision.

If you have had time off from working to raise your children it can feel daunting to return to work. It can feel like you've forgotten all the skills you used to use. If there is something you truly want to do, have faith that you can learn or relearn anything. One of the most consistent problems I see with mothers is a lack of confidence. The world really does feel like it shrinks during early motherhood as we focus our attention on our children. With some confidence and self-belief you can achieve anything! Confidence comes from the mindset we choose, so if you are feeling less than confident you will need to retrain your thinking processes.

If you can't immediately identify your unique gifts and talents speak to your friends and ask what they see in you. Participate in some quiet self-reflection and write a list of all the things you do well or of the experiences that you have had to "cope" with. Your approach to life is unique to you. Look at what you loved in childhood; it can often provide clues. If you are still unsure, think about who you want to be and what gifts and talents you would need …almost anything can be learned if you are willing.

The most important aspect of life is your mindset. Your thoughts help to create your feelings and in combination they send your vibration into the universe. Like attracts like….always! If your thoughts are unclear and unfocused, your direction will not be clear either. Mindset can limit or expand our opportunities in life. A strong mindset is one where we have clear vision, we think happy thoughts and create the feeling as though our vision has already come into being, and we deal in a positive way mentally with any situation that occurs along our journey.

Everyone has a comfort zone, although it may not be comfortable there. Your comfort zone may be that you only just have enough money to cover your bills. To think and feel as though you have an abundance of money is not only foreign but also highly uncomfortable. If you want to create any change you must be willing to step out of the boundaries of comfort you have created. It can be challenging but the end result highly rewarding.

Questions for self-reflection

1.   What gifts and talents do I bring to the world?

_____

_____

_____

_____

_____

2.   What does life purpose mean to me?

_____

_____

_____

_____

_____

3.   What do I need to do to improve my mindset?

_____

_____

_____

_____

_____

CHAPTER 8

WE ARE CREATIVE BEINGS

Creativity is our ability to bring to life what we see in our soul. Let go and have the freedom to create without judgment. Feel the pure joy of creating in whatever form it is that makes your soul sing.

I grew up thinking that I was the "sporty" one and not the "creative" one. I also believed that creativity was about visual art ability and writing. As I grew older, I realized that creativity is about expressing myself, whether through artistic pursuits such as painting and drawing or other forms. I had to change the way I saw creativity to understand that we are all creative beings, including me. That has now given me the freedom to have fun creating.

The process of creation should be fun, free-spirited and all encompassing in the moment. Watching my children, I see some of the most fun times for them are when they are creating paintings, imaginary worlds or stories. The most stimulating school projects are those where they have to create something, whether a picture, power point presentation or iMovie. When they are creating, they have so much more fun and engage more than when they are writing out times tables or spelling words.

Now that I have accepted that I'm a creative being, I have fun creating whatever I feel like. This might range from cooking an amazing dinner to writing a book. I am no longer concerned if other people like what I'm creating; it is a bonus if they do! I used to be scared of showing myself to the world in case people wouldn't like whom I was. It has been most heartwarming for me to show this abundance of love that I have in my heart and feel strong enough not to let others belittle it. I want others to see and experience that feeling. It's only by creating things with confidence and having the courage to express myself out loud and in front of other people that I can share those ideals with everyone.

Watch your children when they are embarking on a journey of creation. They can create anything with a cardboard box. They don't need it to be perfect; to them it can represent whatever they want it to. They don't have doubt about the box not being good enough. Remember, I said everything begins with a thought; this book, your chair, bed, your car, a light bulb! Imagine the satisfaction the creator of those things felt when they saw it coming to life. No matter what we want to create, when we see our creative expression come to life in a physical form it's exciting, fun and it feels good, especially if you don't judge it as being good or bad.

What does creation mean?

It means bringing something into being that wasn't there before. We don't have to sell or make money from what we create (but it's nice if we can). More importantly though, when we create, our imagination comes alive and we can express what our spirit feels. There are two fundamentals to follow when creating:

1. Do not judge what you are creating while in the process – give yourself the freedom to enjoy the process of creating. Once it's complete, you can evaluate and see if there's more you need to learn or improve upon.
2. What you create should not cause harm to others – you want to feel good about what you create, as it's a reflection of you. When we harm others, this says a lot about how we feel about ourselves.

The energy we have when creating something will affect the outcome of our creation. For instance, if we are writing a book from a place of love, the book will turn out very differently from a book we write when in an angry, hurt or guilty space. That's why we should never send a letter or an email written in anger! The same is true when we are creating a painting; the thinking or feeling of the painter becomes obvious through the use of colors, topics, textures, etc.

Creation comes in millions of different forms. Most important is how we feel during the process. Of course, when we see the end result we are likely to judge what we have created. The more you enjoy the process of creating, the better you will feel inside and the less you will care about the outcome. Even when we are doing finger painting with our children we get some astonishing results. Some we will want to keep and others can go straight into the rubbish bin. But it didn't dampen the enjoyment that we had in the process of creating.

Most of us fear the judgment of others and as such keep our creations to ourselves or don't create at all. We do need to have a vision of what we want at the end of the journey, but also to know that we might not create it the first time. It might take us on a journey that we did not expect. Focus on the process and the enjoyment of what you are doing, but have a vision of what you are aiming toward. When Thomas Edison was inventing the light bulb he failed 10,000 times. If, at any moment along that journey, he had stopped and said, "I can't do this," we may not have ended up with the light bulb we have today. He persevered and followed his creative instincts. He didn't see himself as failing 10,000 times. Instead, to his thinking he found 10,000 ways that the light bulb wouldn't work. Now, that is a strong mindset! If we can find that same commitment, passion, energy and enthusiasm, we have the freedom to create anything.

We can explore creativity in many different ways whether we play with our children or build the world's tallest building. Growing up, my sister was extraordinary at writing and drawing pictures. I was not extraordinary at either at that point of my life. I assessed myself and decided I couldn't create anything of value. One of my greatest releases was when my children were young and we began painting. I stopped worrying whether my skills were good or not and just had fun. I bought myself a canvas and painted what I felt like painting and now the finished products hang on our walls. My paintings have an energy and vibrancy that I understand, and I don't care if anyone else likes them. I was able to let go of whether or not I could draw and simply enjoy expressing myself.

We all tend to categorize ourselves and close off possibilities. There are a lot of techniques we can use to stimulate our imagination and creativity. But we need to start with our thinking, to consider how we see creativity and whether we have beliefs that limit our possibilities. It's time to let your imagination run a little wild and step into the freedom of creating whatever it is you want to create.

117

Using your imagination

Using your imagination gets you in touch with another side of yourself and, importantly, it gets your brain active. We tend to get into routines and patterns in our life, but by engaging with our imagination we can create something different. Your brain cannot tell the difference between imagination and reality, so when you dream about whatever you want in your life, your brain thinks it's real. I love to spend time every day visualizing what I want in my life as if it's already here. The more I do that, the more I can feel the universe lining things up. I have found that the more I engage my imagination, even if it's visualizing what I want, the more I want to create things. There's a connection between how much we use our imagination and our will to create.

One thing I love to do is allow my imagination to go where it wants to go. Sometimes, it will lead to creation and other times it will take me on a journey. It is a joy to stimulate my imagination and run a movie through my mind of the things I want in my life and who I want to be. Many of us are told to stop daydreaming and come back to reality - we need to do just the opposite! We need to daydream to engage our imagination, to visualize what we want and then allow the universe to support us in our creation of it. This does not mean we should daydream the entire day and disengage ourselves from life. We need to participate in the life that we have and be fully present, but we also need to use that imagination and allow it to lead us into our creativity. Giving yourself just five minutes every day to visualize what you want begins to stimulate your creativity and imagination.

What would I do if I knew I could do anything?

This is one of the best questions we can ask ourselves because it opens up our imagination to new possibilities. It will also show us where we have blocks and where we limit our thinking. We can identify what we really want and look for ways to support our dreams. When I first asked myself this question, I found that my thinking was quite limited and needed to ask this many times until I felt my possibilities expand. The more you do this exercise the more you can expand your ideas and imagination, because you don't allow any lack of belief to get in your way.

If we have unfulfilled dreams, at some point we need to make a decision about what we want out of life and we need to stop limiting ourselves. This question opens up possibilities; it can help us see our life and the world from a different perspective. It can motivate and inspire us or leave us feeling overwhelmed, generally because we get stuck worrying about the "how". When you're answering this question, let go of how things will happen and just be playful.

What should I create?

There is no right or wrong answer to this for anyone. Whatever your spirit wants to create is what you should create. Don't let anyone else's opinion stand in your way. Get in touch with what you want to bring to the world. Creation and creativity shows up in all forms in our world from artwork, dance and cooking to inventing new machines or even creating ways to be happier within a job that you're in. Imagine you decided that you wanted to create a way for people to be happier within their job – that would open up a whole range of possibilities you'd never thought of before. What you create need not be for other people though; it may simply be for your own enjoyment.

If you have a clear picture of your dreams you will be clearer about what you want to create. Regardless of whether we are conscious of it, we are always creating our own life. However, if our focus is on what we don't want, we will create more of that. Life is generally happier when we are focusing on what we want with an open mind and heart. Allow your imagination to run free, whether it's the big house and the cars, a ranch with horses, building your own school, helping children learn to read, or stopping world hunger.

When two of my children were at school and the youngest was still at home with me, I was the President of our Parents and Citizens Association at the school. I had a vision of a playground for our Year 4-7 children because they didn't have one. They had a sports field to play on and their school had beautiful grounds with kangaroos appearing regularly. But my goal was to see this playground come to life. In my vision it was a big playground and we would need at least $90,000 to build it. It took three years and a very interesting journey to see that playground become a reality. At first, I didn't know how we would fund it, I just knew I wanted it. Now, when I see the children running over and playing on it, it gives me great satisfaction.

A project for me!

A project or series of projects are a great way to start creating the life of our dreams. We can start with a small project to achieve the feeling of success and increase our confidence. If you would like to engage your creativity to increase your productiveness and work toward the life of your dreams you will need to take some action. When you break your dream into small "next step" projects, it becomes less overwhelming. You start to see cycles of action that are easier to follow all the way through. This will help to develop your mindset, increase your confidence and see some progress.

I invite you to choose a small project, whether it's to scrapbook your children's photos or build a playground at their school. Choose a project you would like to start working on that you believe will engage your creativity and imagination, then take the first step. A fun way to do this is to give yourself a 30-day challenge. When you look back on those 30 days you will see that something changed: you created something. It's very satisfying and, of course, if you do 12 of those 30-day challenges in a year, you find that you have created at least 12 things in one year. Bigger projects will take longer, but you can divide those bigger projects into 30-day challenges. The idea of a challenge is to motivate you to engage with your creativity and to get you to take some action. Think about a project you might like to do. Make sure it's in alignment with you and your family and that it is something you will feel good about. Break the project into small steps and commit to a little each day. Let go of any judgment about what you want to do and allow your imagination to run wild.

Think about your needs and what you would like in your life. A lot of my projects involve my children because I want to work with them and spend time with them. We have a lot of fun when we embark on a family project and when we start to see results it gives us all confidence and brings us closer together. The project might also be something you want to work on with your friends. When we have the mastermind effect (a group of people all working together on the same thing), we are far more powerful and can motivate and inspire each other to stay on track and achieve whatever the vision is for our project. When I was fundraising for my children's school I felt a lot of satisfaction because I knew it was helping the children and the school; it gave me a sense of purpose. Choose a project that makes your heart sing, that makes you feel good.

What does my ego say?

If you listen to your ego, it will tell you that you are not good enough, not smart enough, that you don't have the resources and that you can't possibly achieve what you want. The more you listen to that little voice that says you can't do it, the more you hold yourself back. If we can recognize that the little voice is simply our ego, we can choose not to listen. When my ego kicks in, I will say, "Thanks for your opinion, but I am going to do this anyway."

Think about how you want to live the rest of your life. If you want to live thinking that you can't do things, you are free to do so, but be aware that it is a disempowered way of living. Use the tools in Chapter 2 to turn negative into positive thoughts. You will have opportunities to use those tools every day, but start by being aware of what you are thinking and when your ego kicks in. Pretty much anytime when you are being judgmental of yourself or other people, if you are making negative comments or having negative thoughts, you will be in ego. Generally we find it harder to recognize our ego when we are in self-doubt because we are so used to functioning that way. When we come from our essence, from our true spirit, we know that we are all equal as human beings and that everyone has gifts and talents to bring into this world. As soon as we are not feeling that, we have slid from essence into the world of ego.

Leaping into your essence

In our essence we see the perfection of life and can listen to our heart. It is where we see our children as perfect beings even if their behavior is not. It is when we see our partner as the beautiful person she/he is and see ourselves as a beautiful, productive, vital human being. For some of you this might sound like a fairytale. But we can choose to see the world from this viewpoint and when we do, there is a wonderful sense of peace about life.

We can enjoy the fact that we are on a journey and we do not necessarily know where we want to go yet. When we are in essence we can let go of the desire to control others, and we allow everyone to discover who they really are. Our essence understands that everything is part of the journey and contributes to the experience we have on earth. In saying that, there are people who experience great life challenges and situations that we would not wish on anyone. Yet these people can become our biggest inspiration when we watch them overcome and live a vital life.

We are vulnerable and risk being hurt when we show our essence. As children this happened many times, which taught us to hide our true self. When we feel secure about who we are and what we bring to the world, we can come from a place of love and the world will reflect that love back to us. We can create the experiences, and meet the people we want to have in our lives. We can create a social group that we feel connected to, who supports and encourages us. When we operate out of ego we attract just the opposite. We can attract negative experiences and situations that do not make us feel good.

Almost always when we are angry, we are in ego and we don't see life from our heart or the situation from a bigger perspective. I know this can be very challenging, especially with our children. I have challenges with my children when they are not behaving in the way I think they should. I can feel myself getting angry and sometimes yell at them, and other times I will be able to catch myself and ask what is happening within me. A lot of the time when our children are misbehaving it is because they need something that they cannot express. The more I get in tune with understanding the idea of ego and essence, the better I feel as a parent.

The experience you will find when you re-discover your essence is gentleness, a discovery that you actually have ability to approach every situation from love. It takes time to live more from essence than ego, but the end result is absolutely worth it.

Uh-oh, I'm sabotaging myself again.

Self-sabotage is something almost everyone does and it comes from a place of ego and fear. Sometimes I even hear people say, "this can't last" or "something has to go wrong soon." As soon as we move to this lower vibrational way of thinking, we start to see things go wrong. Few people are used to living in a way that they love, and in which life flows easily. Generally, people are used to struggle and this has become a comfort zone for many people in the world. When life begins to move in the direction we want, we will often sabotage that. That sabotage comes in many different forms. It may be in our thinking, feelings or actions. Whatever it is, it can turn our vision into a nightmare, from a situation of hope into a hopeless one…in our mind.

If we can remember that we have the power to be, do or have anything, then as soon as we are thinking otherwise, we can recognize it as sabotage. Our old belief patterns can be one of our greatest saboteurs. One of the ways I used to sabotage myself was to create something in my work, then decide it wasn't good enough. I would share it with people and even if it made a difference, I would see it as a failure. I can see now this had a lot do with the comfort zone I was in and my beliefs about my skills and talents.

Now that I am focused on my goals, I want to make sure that I'm not sabotaging myself. I make sure I am supporting myself in whatever way I need to so my goal can come into being. I now understand that I have value, that I bring love into this world and that it's my right to create whatever I want and have fun while doing it. As you define the vision you want for your life, notice how you might be sabotaging that vision. The more aware you are of how you function in the world, the more you can steer your thoughts and feelings in a positive direction.

Techniques to shift into essence

Radiating Love Vibration

When radiating love, we can't help but step out of ego. Love is the highest vibration in the universe, and you cannot stay in a negative emotional state when you are radiating love. This simple exercise will make you feel better and add to the positive vibration in the world. Just sit quietly and feel love in your heart. Allow that love to spread throughout your body. Imagine the love spreading out through your heart area and into the room you are in, your community, city, state, country and eventually the entire world. Sit in this feeling for as long as you want – it may be one minute or fifteen minutes. Then gently bring that feeling of love back through the same pathway into your heart. Notice the difference in your energy and how much calmer you feel. When you connect with that feeling of love and expand it into the world, you will move out of ego and contribute to a different energy in the world. You also begin to get in touch with the power that exists within you.

Breathing into essence

Breathing is one of the most centering exercises we can do. Few people in the world breathe properly. We tend to breathe shallowly into our lungs, rather than deeply into our abdomen. When breathing into essence, your focus is upon slowing your breathing down. Become aware of your breath, lengthen the inward breath, then extend your outward breath. Put your hand on your stomach and make sure you are breathing into your abdomen, not just into your lungs. You might want to close your eyes because it feels good and you may feel yourself slip into a different space. As you focus on your breath, allow anything that's bothering you to gently slip away. This is a great exercise if you're feeling angry or hurt...or anything else that is causing you to feel disconnected from essence.

Chapter Summary

Part of our journey on this earth is to experience the power of creation. Yet many of us feel we are not creative because of our preconceptions of creativity. Creation is simply bringing something into existence, that wasn't there before. Every day we are creative in the way we think and act. There is much joy in bringing something physical into the world that comes from you.

The two fundamentals of creation are: don't judge yourself and what you create along the way and don't create anything that causes harm to others. By taking the judgment out, you can simply enjoy the process of creating.

Our brain does not distinguish between reality and imagination, so engage the imagination more. It can help to release more of those "happy" chemicals into the body from our brain. Stimulating your imagination will assist you in being more creative, defining new ideas and possibilities for your life…and it's fun! Spend at least five minutes a day imagining what you want in your life.

If you knew you could do anything and wouldn't fail what would you do? Answer this question at least once a week and watch how your imagination expands. New ideas come to you and what you believe as possible will expand.

You are free to create anything you want in life – that is why we have free will. It is totally your choice whether it's something that helps others or is personal to you. It may help to find yourself a project. Anything that inspires you and stimulates your imagination is a great start. As you successfully complete your project you will start to feel more confident. A great way to begin a project is to set a 30-day project, something you know you will enjoy. At the end of 30 days you can look back and see you have achieved something.

If you are hearing any part of your being suggesting you can't do something or you are not good enough, you are in ego. Our ego loves to challenge us and tell us things that simply aren't true. If you listen to your essence (or your heart) you will hear a different, more supportive voice. This voice knows that we are all equal and have equal capacity for building our dream life. Again you choose the voice to which you would prefer to listen.

We all have patterns of self-sabotage for many reasons. We may have developed strong underlying beliefs in childhood that keep us from fulfilling our potential. We may even sabotage on a more conscious level – drinking lots of alcohol to reduce our feeling of dissatisfaction with life or eating foods that we know are not good for our body. There are many ways to self-sabotage. Start by noticing any thoughts that immediately pop into your head and check to see if they are keeping you feeling small.

Two techniques that will help you move into essence are the Radiating Love Vibration technique and Breathing into Essence. Both will help you shift out of the daily grind and remind you of the lighter side of life. There is joy and love to be had in every day and both of these techniques will help you move into these states.

Questions for self-reflection

1. What is one thing I would like to create in my life?

_____

_____

_____

_____

_____

2. What would I do if I could do anything and knew I wouldn't fail?

_____

_____

_____

_____

_____

3. How do I choose to live more fully from my essence?

_____

_____

_____

_____

_____

CHAPTER 9

YOU CAN'T MANAGE YOUR TIME, ONLY YOUR PRIORITIES

We don't get time back – once it's gone it's gone. As we only have a relatively short time on this earth and there is a lot to experience, let's make the most of the time we have here.

It has taken me a lifetime to understand the way that I function in the world. I am highly energetic, I get a lot done in a day, I am constantly in action and I thrive on variety. I realized though that I would distract myself by being busy, but my actions didn't necessarily move me closer to my dreams. I completed many successful projects, but didn't understand that some of those projects were distracting me from what I really wanted to do in life. It wasn't until I understood that I can't manage time, only my priorities, that I then started to change the way that I functioned in the world and I started seeing different results, which was very exciting.

As I take you through this chapter, I invite you to look at your life differently from the way you do now. When my children first started school I was trying to manage time. I would have six hours from the time when they were dropped off at school to when they needed to be picked up. Within that time I had a long list of all of the things I needed to do. That dilemma still exists, but the way I use that time while they are at school has changed greatly because of the concept I present here.

What is time?

Time is simply a form of measurement in our world. It's the way we measure the earth rotating on its axis relative to the sun – one day; the earth orbiting the sun – one year. We also divide the year into seasons depending on whether it's hot or cold. Time is really just a way to measure what's happening on the earth and what's happening with our position relative to the sun. It's a concept that man has formulated to help us relate to our life in terms of past, present and future.

Why you can't manage time

In a marketing course I took years ago, I remember learning time management skills. We were taught all types of techniques to make the most of each day and fit as much in as possible. This keeps the illusion of thinking that we are getting things done and making progress. However, no matter how well you "manage time" you will never get it back and you will never have more time – there will always be 24 hours in a day. Relate this to managing money; if we manage our money well we can make it go further, we can save, we can spend less or more depending upon how we decide to manage it.

What you can do is manage your priorities during a certain period of time. Priorities are those activities that are most important to you. For years I was so busily achieving things and I felt fulfilled for a while because I was hitting some great goals and using my time well... or so I thought. But I was not moving any closer to my dreams. I would allocate time toward those priorities in my role as a mother; in particular a lot of time would get spent trying to make sure that things were in order – cooking, cleaning, washing, etc. When I understood that I needed to prioritize those activities that would move me toward my dreams, I could make sure that I actually took some of those actions every day. Otherwise I would find days would fly by without having done anything for myself. Now, those other tasks I used to focus on still manage to get done as well.

I have found that we need to know what is important to us and to have a vision of how we spend our days. After defining my priorities, I became more focused in my actions and had to let go of some things that I had thought were important but didn't move me toward my dreams. When you undertake a 30-day challenge you will likely have to change some of your priorities because you will have to give energy and time to your project or it won't be completed within that 30-day period. That's why allocating a period of time to your priority can be so powerful: you begin to move forward on a project or your dream. Only you can decide what your priorities are and what is most important to you. Go back to that vision you have for your life – what does the picture look like with your children in it? Life has an interesting way of showing us what should be important to us. For example, when we become ill, we prioritize our health.

Your priorities will most likely change as you grow and as your children grow older. When they are babies, our priority is to keep them clean, dry, fed and to give them enough sleep. Once children are at school the priorities change to include homework, after school activities, etc. All of a sudden, getting up early and getting to school on time happens because it becomes a priority. Life changes again as the children grow older and go to high school because they can manage more for themselves. You may start to see different possibilities open up for yourself at this time. Again, this comes down to your vision and beliefs.

When children go off to school, many mothers look at those few hours as their time to get everything done, just as I did myself. This can lead to getting stuck in a cycle in which finding extra time becomes difficult. When we manage our priorities we change the amount of time we allocate to different activities because we have clarity about what we want to do and achieve in our life. Think about what you are spending your time doing and whether it is in alignment with the life you want to live.

What's important to me as a person?

Considering your life outside of motherhood can give you clarity about what is important to you as a person independently of what is important to you as a mother. We tend to think about our children and families, how they fit into our picture and how whatever we do impacts on them. When you begin to see what is important to you as a person you open up to more possibilities, allowing more of that in your life.

Health and fitness have always been important to me, as has trying new things. At one point when I had one child in school and the other two at home with me, I decided that I wanted to do something that was just for me, and I took up athletics. I hadn't done athletics before other than in high school, and my eldest child was in a club. I liked the variety of trying new events and it had the physical fitness aspect that I wanted. So I became a member of the club where my daughter competed and started training. I enjoyed dedicating time to an activity that was for me. In Australia at a "masters" level (anyone over 35 years) there are not many people who participate in athletics. I found that I wasn't particularly good at any one event and I didn't have any particular strength, but I was okay at everything (I've always been an all-rounder!)

I would travel to competitions on a Saturday morning to participate. You could choose your events; I chose different things every week just to try out various activities. The year I began athletics, the National Master's Athletic championships were held in Brisbane, close to where I lived. I thought I might as well enter and see what happens. I had no expectations but was interested in the experience. I entered myself in the heptathlon, which consists of seven events. This made sense given I was okay at all events but a master of none of them. I competed in my age group and enjoyed the entire experience. I laugh heartily when I look back on this experience because I won the silver medal at those Australian championships. It was my first year ever participating in athletics and I had never done athletics in any form before other than at school. Here I was winning a silver medal...I laugh because there were only two of us competing in that event! It would have made no difference to me if more people had been involved and the result was different because it was so much fun and so fulfilling for me at that time. It was something I was doing just for me!

As you formulate your life vision, think about what you would like to have in your life as a woman, even if it's something as simple as having a pedicure every month. If you choose not to consider your own needs, no one else will either, and you will begin to believe you have no control over your life. It can feel disempowering, like you have no choices any more. I'm not saying there is anything you have to do, but having some sort of dream and vision will feel more empowering and you will feel that you are working towards something.

You can always choose to make time for yourself. This is a part of your mindset about the way you perceive life and whether you are willing to commit some time to your dreams. It may mean devoting only 10 minutes a day to whatever you want. Any change you make needs to come from inside you. Your next step is not about trying to find a quick fix or going to get a part-time job you dislike even though on the surface that might suit the family.

Do I need to change anything?

Unless you are living the life of your dreams, you are happy every day and have goals to work toward it's worth making some changes. There is no requirement to do this; we are all free to choose to live the way we want. However, if you have picked up this book there probably are some things that you would like to change. It can feel a little frightening or even overwhelming to know where to start. I suggest two things:

1. Get a clear vision of what you do want in your life
2. Start to notice and change your thoughts

If you don't create a vision you will have no direction. If you don't change your thoughts you will keep getting the same results. For example, if you think you don't have time to bring in change or follow your dreams, your experience will be one of having no time. If you think that what you want is impossible to reach, then it will stay out of reach. You may need some assistance in this from a coach, mentor, healer, success group or other. When our thinking isn't right we will sabotage ourselves due to these thoughts and our deep-seated beliefs.

When making changes, it is important to understand that you don't have to change everything at once; you can make changes step by step. We didn't expect our children to start walking from day one; we knew that they would sit then crawl, start pulling themselves up and then they would walk. It's exactly the same for us! As we are making changes, we just do it little by little and as we take those steps, we allow our children and our family to grow with us. Some of you will make a decision and dive head first into change. Be aware that your thinking is not necessarily aligned with your children or your partner's thoughts; they may need more time to adjust. When I make a decision, I tend to go at it like a tornado and all of a sudden I am creating a change and dragging people with me. I have to remind myself to invite my children to come on the journey with me because I really want them there and sometimes that change in them doesn't come quite as quickly as I expected.

If you have identified some dreams that you want to incorporate in your life, then you will need to prioritize them. You will need to consider how you spend your time each day and focus some energy on those activities that move you toward your vision. This is not rocket science – if you keep doing the same things, you will keep getting the same results. If you want things to change, then you have to change the way you do things and what you are doing. Many mothers I have spoken with feel they don't have time to do take different actions, move toward their goals, or even to work on a project. The days seem to fly by. I remember looking back and wondering what I did with my day when my children arrived home from school. As my goals in life and my priorities became clearer, I chose to focus my attention and make sure that I was spending some time every day "doing" things that would move in the direction I want to go.

Begin by making small changes; start prioritizing one thing you want to see more of in your life. You will find that you will feel happier when you allocate time for things that are important to you. If it doesn't make you feel happier it's safe to assume that the action you're taking is not pointing in the right direction for you. Often I have found that when people tell me they don't have time to do something it's an excuse because they don't know how to do it or they are afraid of the consequences. They are unsure of their ability to do it and are afraid they might fail, so they fall back on the excuse of time. The reality is that most people spend time on things that are not serving them, such as watching television. If you would rather watch television than work toward your dreams that is a choice, but be honest about it to yourself. If you have other priorities that stop you from doing the things you want to, notice these choices and take responsibility for them. You will not create change without giving up some activities but if your end goal is worth it nothing will stop you.

Feeling in balance

Periodically, I reevaluate the balance I want in my life. I said earlier we never find ideal balance but we can define what balance is for us and what it looks like. We all need to have some rest and relaxation time, but how much we need differs from one person to the next. Some of the time we spend resting or relaxing can be spent productively working toward our dreams. I can see mothers raising their eyebrows at the idea of resting and relaxing – maybe for you it's letting go of having to do all the cooking, cleaning or having some time with your children. Remember that balance doesn't really exist and no matter how much we chase it, there are always things we want to do that we can't fit in. I know people will find this notion confronting – I can only share that my experience of letting go of trying to find balance and focusing on the things I love has been freeing and empowering. I have so much that I want to get done and experience in my life that it will never look like a balanced life to anyone else. Yet I'm happy and fulfilled … when you think about balance ask yourself what is so attractive about it. Why do you want it and what's the feeling you think being in "balance" will give you?

Most of the time we feel happier when we are moving toward our dreams. When we can see that the vision of our family fits in with this dream, we are going to feel really good. When we focus on being balanced we take the focus off our dream. I can hear people say, "My dream is to live a balanced life!" I wonder why anyone would want balance because there is so much fun to be had – I'd like to have an outrageous amount of fun, not a balanced amount. I have no intention of ever being balanced in my life. If balance is important to you though consider why it's important and what you believe will change if your life is in balance. I'm not saying you have to give up on balance, just maybe look at it in a different way. Then again, you may disagree with this idea. It's never for anyone else to say what balance should look like – the decision is entirely yours.

Taking care of them, taking care of you

Our vision as mothers tends to either include the children or it's a vision we believe possible for us when our children are in a different stage of life. If we focus on how things will happen, it might be difficult to define a vision that includes the children as well as us successfully achieving our dreams. We all love our children and along our journey we will find a way to give our children what they need. They will learn to embrace our dreams and vision and they may learn a few lessons along the way. We always want to look after our children as mothers but by doing so, we don't need to forget our own dreams. The closer we become to who we want to be, the more we can share our essence with our children. You may end up feeling more connected with your children because you will sense they love you as a whole being and not just as someone who does everything for them.

Many will recognize the situation – if you're not happy the whole house ends up being unhappy! We have a right to find fulfillment and to pursue our own happiness, whatever that looks like and means to us. Happiness is not something that we should compromise. Many of you are not necessarily unhappy and you may well be happy enough. Yet most people have ideas about what they would like to change; the main reason is that they believe they will be happier once the change has occurred. If this is you, then it's time to start dreaming again, to create some future plans for yourself. Work out what the absolutes are for you, those things you won't compromise. Then you can get clear about the things you are willing to give up. For me, some of those compromises are that I want my children to live with me, to have quality time with them, and to be there for their sports, concerts, etc. But I am learning to let go of other things as well such as doing all the household chores myself (they are old enough to help now!), giving them time and space without me or allowing someone else to drive them to training sessions.

Many mothers can't answer when I ask them what they do to look after themselves. This is because their entire focus has been around family and children, making sure everyone else's needs are met. I am asking you to look at your life and consider what you are doing for yourself to nurture and take care of you. There are structures and beliefs in our society that might make us feel like it's selfish to consider what we want for ourselves. If we can break through those barriers and beliefs that have been set up and challenge what we believe about what it means to take care of ourselves, we can open up possibilities and bring in more of what we really want in our heart.

Is fun a priority for me?

The way I see life, fun should be a priority for everyone. We need to have fun; we need to laugh because it makes us feel good. When I ask a lot of mothers what they do for fun, they look at me like I'm an alien. Their day is full of work when the kids are at school, and when they come home, there's homework, sports, music and routines to make sure they are fed on time and in bed on time. Routine is wonderful and helps kids feel secure, but we also need to fit our own fun into that routine. A lot of us have forgotten what fun is and what it feels like to us. I invite you have a look at the fun in your life. Is it something that you only have on a weekend or a Friday night? Is there something that you can do every day that feels like fun?

Laughter is the greatest medicine we can give ourselves; I encourage you all to laugh as much as you can. Children laugh a lot more than adults. Once we became adults, life became more serious. Things we used to find funny are no longer amusing to us and we have all these things in the background that are worrying us. When we laugh it stimulates our organs through the increase in air we take in and it causes our brain to produce endorphins that make us feel good.

It should always feel good

The key to life is feeling good and we must aim to feel good in every moment. If we don't feel good, then our job is to feel better. If this is the only thing you get out of this book then you have received wonderful value! When you feel good and love yourself, you will have people in your life that you want to be around; people who support you and love you. Feeling good comes from the inside; there is nothing that you need from the outside world or anyone else to feel good. The way we feel is a choice we make in every moment. It's a disempowering view to believe that we need to rely on someone else or for something to happen to feel good.

We are human beings and we are supposed to feel an entire range of emotions, and there will be times when we don't feel good. But if you're not feeling good the majority of the time, you need to look at where you're giving away your power and why you're choosing to feel bad. Ask anyone with depression – all they want is to feel good again. If I know I have a challenging day ahead I write in my journal "feel good today," or "laugh lots today" because I know I might need remind myself to feel good. It is always our responsibility how we feel.

When I talk about feeling good, I don't mean pretending to the world that we feel good like a mask when something else is going on inside. As women, we often put our own needs aside and pretend that everything's okay. If everything isn't okay our first priority is to go gently, love ourselves and take baby steps to feeling better. The more we can do that, the more we can shift into a higher vibration and start to feel good. Use the emotional scale in Chapter 5 to look at where you are emotionally and where you want go. Keep your focus on feeling good no matter what because situations will occur and life will happen.

What is a universal manager?

One system that I use that has helped me so much in letting go of needing to control everything is to hand tasks/dreams over to the universe. In my way of thinking, it allows the universe to support me and for me to feel supported. I don't know how things will happen, but I have a clear dream. The idea that we have control over everything is an illusion we have been brought up to believe. Our response to situations is the only thing we can control; we don't control the situation but through our energy we do influence it. Life rarely works out the way we think it will. When we let go of control, we allow other people to step up and the universe to make things happen that we couldn't predict. I liken it to putting my wish out to the universe; the universe then turns all the cogs and wheels to make things happen.

I have learnt to trust there are things happening for me that I don't know about; feeling this takes a lot of pressure off me needing to do everything to make my dream come true. Think back to a time when you worked in a group, whether in a family, a committee, or a club. We get more done and achieve a better result if we are all working together as a mastermind. For those who have had bad experiences working in a group, this is most likely because the group did not have a cohesive vision. I feel that each day I create a mini-mastermind with the universe, it keeps me focused on my intentions.

The Journal System…

I use a personalized dairy system, using a plain journal book. Every morning I write my intentions for the day … but in a different way to most people. The headings I use are:

1. **Universal Manager:** Here I list anything that I want the universe to take care of. These might be meeting people to help me along my journey, things I'd like to see happen in my life or the world or anything else! Once I've written them down I don't think about them again – they have been handed over. At some point later I might get an intuition to take some action but for today it's done with. For example, as I am writing a book I could ask for someone to help with the cover design. In writing it down, I'm allowing the universe to start putting in motion the actions it needs to fulfill what it is that I want. I know for some people this may seem a bit far-fetched, but I can tell you that this is working for me. I see examples every day of things coming to life that I've handed over to the Universal Manager. It has also allowed me to focus my activities and renew my dream every day. I found this difficult at first though because I was so used to thinking I had to control and do everything.

2. **Priority Manager:** This is where I list my tasks for the day. Some of these actions will be moving me toward my dreams and some will be about more mundane chores. I don't write as long a list as I used to when I used a "to do"

list. Instead, I only include the most important actions. For example, I might note the action to write one chapter of my book along with exercise, listening to a motivational audio, etc. Depending on my mood I might even write how I want to feel that day. When writing your priorities make sure there is at least one thing on the list that is moving you toward your dreams.

When I first started writing my priorities I wrote actions such as defining my dreams and creating a vision board. Once those were clear, I had a better idea of what actions to take, what my next logical step should be. Nowadays, I only know what my step is for today. I can't know what the next two months, years or decade holds, but I trust that when I need to know, I will know. For now I focus on what I want to get done for the day. I can refer back to the list throughout the day to help keep me on track. I find it a great motivational tool.

3. **Gratitude:** Here I write what I'm grateful for in my life because the attitude of gratitude sets me up for a wonderful day. When you are focused on the things in your life that you feel great about and that are already working for you, you start to feel good. And the more you feel good the more you will attract more of those things to feel grateful for.

4. **Achievements & Success:** At the end of a day in the same journal I write down my achievements and my successes for the day. This means that, every day, I focus on what I've done and on my achievements. When we do this we start to see every day as successful, rather than focusing on what we didn't get done or how much more we have to get done. By acknowledging and recognizing that we have ticked off some important priorities, we begin to feel confident and successful. If we find that our achievements and successes are things we have done but that don't relate to our priority manager (or dreams), then we've got an indication of where our focus is or isn't.

Using this journal system will help to motivate and inspire you, keep you focused on your priorities and to determine whether the actions you take in a day are the important ones.

Chapter Summary

Man created time to measure the earth's activity relative to the sun. We tend to think we can manage time, but we can't manage it because no matter how much we try we will not get more than 24 hours a day. We can stay distracted from our dreams for years trying to manage our time better.

If you know who you are and what you truly love, then you can live the values that are important to you. It's very difficult to prioritize if you are not clear about those values. If you want to make your dreams come true then you will need to make sure you know what your priorities are. Remember you are a person as well as a mother and there may be some ideas lurking in your mind, ready to be shown to the world. No one "has" to make change in his or her life. But if you want a different, better and happier life you will need to change. And it begins with changing your thinking.

Many modern texts tell us to strive for "balance" in life. We are told that balance is important and that we will feel better if life is in balance. So we try to achieve this in all areas of our lives. However, the more you aim at doing what makes you happy, the less you think about balance because you will feel so good - you won't have the traditional idea of balance. There is too much fun in the world to be had to hide behind our idea of balance.

Your children will always be a priority. Yet as a woman you need to find some space to relax and be someone other than a mother. Fun is a part of that and is totally underrated as an adult. There are all forms and methods of having fun and some will appeal to you more than others. Whatever it is that makes you smile and laugh, do more of it!

Almost everything we do should feel good to us. If you aren't feeling good about something, that's the vibrations you are sending into the universe…and then you start to create more things that don't feel good. It is more productive to focus on moving yourself into a better emotional state and then let your thoughts roam free.

The daily diary system I use incorporates my priorities, my wishes and dreams, and letting go of control. In the morning I write in 3 sections; Universal Manager, Gratification and Priority Manager. I hand all the unknowns over to the Universal Manager e.g.: physical wants and needs, people I'd like to run into and anything that I don't know how will come into my life. The second section "Gratification" has me focus on all the wonderful things in my life that I have to feel grateful for. An attitude of gratitude goes a long way. Lastly I use the Priority Manager – this is to determine what I need to focus on during the day and gives me a reference point. At the end of the day I write all of my Achievements and Successes for the day, which leaves me feeling that I am a success and that I've taken steps each day towards my dream.

Questions for self-reflection

1. What's most important to me as a person?

_____

_____

_____

_____

_____

2. What things do I allow to get in my way of creating what I want?

_____

_____

_____

_____

_____

3. How can I use my diary to focus upon my dreams or my project?

_____

_____

_____

_____

_____

CHAPTER 10

MAKE A DECISION

We all have to decide what we want out of life. Not deciding is a choice we make out of fear, but it leaves us feeling victim to life's circumstances.

Every day we make hundreds of decisions, from what we are going to wear, what to cook and where we are going through to go, to whom we will be talking to during that day. The decisions I discuss in this chapter are those that will create change in your life, those that will move you to your dream and will bring more of what you want into your life. As I focus more on my dreams and what I want to do, there are certain activities, beliefs and thoughts that I have had to give up. I have chosen to give them up because I know that they are not helping me move toward my dreams.

When our TV set broke down the decision not to buy another one was easy because I did not want to have that sort of distraction in my house. A much bigger decision was when I chose to get a divorce; I knew that to stay wasn't going to fulfill me in the way that I wanted in this life. Even though it was a hard decision, I knew I needed to make it. Now I am more conscious of my decisions each day, if my choices reflect the person I want to be and whether they move me in the direction I want. I take responsibility for how I choose to use my time, the priorities I set for myself and even for how big I allow myself to dream. When you understand the importance and value of making a decision and making a commitment to work toward what you want, your mindset changes. People who procrastinate waste a lot of time and energy, watching and waiting for some signal that will assure them of making the "right" decision. It is empowering to make a decision and take responsibility for the outcome. Only when you have decided what you want out of life can you focus your attention on that and make decisions that are in alignment with your aims.

Some of your decisions may not have taken you in the "right" direction. That is, they may not have produced the outcome you expected. However, there is always good in every decision even if it's only clarifying what you don't want, and you can always change course by making a new decision. It's much like a ship – if the captain finds it has gone off course, she will adjust it until it's back on track towards its destination. We are constantly adjusting our course in life; however, for many of us it's quite unconscious. If we do not have a dream or a vision for our life, we make decisions based on our momentary emotional state and do what appears to be most logical from that point of view.

I highly recommend making a vision board and populating it with pictures that represent what you want in your life. Put it in a place where you can see it all the time and let it inspire your decisions. Equally of value is a dream book – a book you can carry with you with pictures of things that you want in life. When you do this and you start collecting pictures, it stimulates your imagination. It's a powerful motivator and it gives you focus. If you are not sure about what you want to do, understand that where you are right now is just a moment in time and that it will become clearer if you ask yourself questions. Throughout life, when you don't know what to do, notice the things you don't like and use them to clarify what you do want.

Decisions made from a sense of pressure or fears are generally due to the lack of a clear vision of where we are going. For me, outcomes are much better when I have clarity and I follow my heart. It is so important to make decisions with the right mindset, an open heart and to know that there is no pressure to be right. Decisions carry consequences and we have to take responsibility for them. However, there are not many outcomes that we can't turn around into positive consequences. It is most important that we make decisions and act upon them. When we make no decisions at all, we begin to stagnate. If there is some change you want to make but you are not quite sure what it looks like, start with something that feels like it's low pressure. Make little changes, step by step. Change anything that will create a positive shift in your vibration. Lighten up and enjoy the process and allow your decisions to take you on a journey.

If you are truly unclear about what you want in life, your starting point must be to seek clarity. Gather pictures, use a journal and visualize the details of how you would like life to look. Don't worry about how these things will happen. Pictures will start to make your dreams clearer and more tangible. For example: if you want to have family holidays, choose pictures that represent that to you. For now start with something, any decision that will move you closer to what you want. If you can commit to answering the questions throughout this book, you will find that you begin to make some of the changes that you want, even if the big picture is still very vague.

I don't have to get it right now

It is okay if you don't see your big picture clearly yet. You don't have to know every detail of it. As you continue the journey, you will find these details grow and change as you do. When making decisions, it is important to remember that we are allowed to make mistakes along the way. What we call mistakes are simply unexpected outcomes. The more we give ourselves permission to be on a journey, the less fear we have around making decisions. We all love to be right, but life simply is not like that. Treat the mistakes you make as a valuable lesson on how not to do something, the same as Thomas Edison did when he was inventing the light bulb. Our fear of making mistakes can inhibit our trust in intuition. If you can trust that any outcome will eventually work out better for you, you will feel more comfortable using your intuition for making decisions.

Changing your routine

Any step, no matter how big or small, is going to be the beginning of your journey of change. Making small adjustments to a routine begins to shift our mindset, thoughts and habits. You might drive a different way to work or school, cook different meals, or begin a new form of exercise – anything that will move you out of your regular pattern of behavior. Most of us have such fixed routines that we have become creatures of habit. One week doesn't look very different from another and time just passes. Is your life a repetition of the previous week – the same thing each day and evening with some slight differences on weekends? Changing your routine tells the inner you that there are things you can do right now even if you don't know what those bigger decisions are. Making small changes successfully gives you confidence and creates a cycle of success. If you want to make big changes, go for it, but just make sure that you have a clear picture of what you want and that your mindset, beliefs and feelings are devoted to your purpose and goal. I have found that changing my routine doesn't throw off my kids as much as I think it will. In fact, they can embrace the change and it becomes a new normal very quickly.

Decision Paralysis

Decision paralysis is a state in which we don't make a decision – when we are either stopped by fear or we just don't know what the right decision is. Instead we refrain from making any decisions, hoping that, by some miracle, life will simply work out. This keeps us so disempowered, for we start to believe that life is "happening to us". This can lead to a victim mentally of learned helplessness. When we don't make a decision, it keeps us in limbo and feels like our dreams will never come true. If you have goals you would like to achieve, you only ever need to make a decision about your one next step. Once you've taken a step the next step will become clearer. Be conscious about what you are thinking and what you are choosing at every moment. You always have the choice not to make a decision. There will be times when you need to wait, but most of the time when we fail to make that decision it is because we are paralyzed by fear.

Fear can hide itself in many different disguises. It can have us making excuses for things, we can waste time weighing up decisions, or we tell ourselves it is not the right time yet. Remember that FEAR (False Evidence Appearing Real) is an illusion that exists in our mind if we allow it. However, many of us succumb to it, and it can be an overriding driver of our life. Many people think it is the fear of failure that holds us back. Most of the time, though, it's a fear of success that stops us because we are not used to seeing ourselves as successful; we don't know who we will be if we succeed at what we want to achieve.

One my favorite quotes explains this simply and perfectly:

"Our deepest fear is not that we are inadequate. Our deepest fear is that we are powerful beyond measure. It is our light, not our darkness that most frightens us. We ask ourselves, who am I to be brilliant, gorgeous, talented, fabulous? Actually, who are you not to be? You are a child of God. Your playing small does not serve the world. There is nothing enlightened about shrinking so that other people won't feel insecure around you. We are all meant to shine, as children do. We were born to make manifest the glory of God that is within us. It's not just in some of us; it's in everyone. And as we let our own light shine, we unconsciously give other people permission to do the same. As we are liberated from our own fear, our presence automatically liberates others"

Marianne Williamson

The media does its best to keep us in a fear cycle of not being "good enough" or being "unworthy". We are shown artificial images of perfection instead of recognizing natural beauty that exists within all of us. Through a school system that grades us according to what we "should" be able to do we are told whether we are average, below average or above average. We are taught through the reactions of others that getting things wrong means we're stupid or not worthy. All of these add up to create beliefs within us that it is bad to make mistakes. Yet, some of our greatest experiences occur when we are wrong. Some people I have met on my journey because I got it "wrong" have turned out to be great friends; my mistakes have taught me such a lot about life and human nature. To have the courage to make mistakes we need to trust that everything is happening for our good or that everything will work out.

If we find ourselves off course we can change the way we are doing something until we get it right or find another way it works. In life, there are very few decisions that that will put us so far off course that we can't get back. Some of the most inspiring people in this world today went off course and found their way. Mistakes were part of their journey and their story, but their mistakes don't define who they are. Our response tells us more about who we are than the actual mistake. A gentler approach to life is to allow your self to make mistakes, take notice of decisions you've made and learn from them.

What makes sense in my life?

In the end it doesn't matter what anyone else thinks about your life, but what YOU think of your life matters greatly. As a mother, most of the time what you think is right will be guided in some part by your family. Learn to trust that the inner you knows what is right for you and what will make you happy. You can ask your friends - they will all give different opinions. Ever had the experience of asking friends for their advice, none of which appeals to you or feels right for you? That's because inside you already know what is right for you.

Determining your direction is about following your own internal guidance. Your guidance might not make sense to your logical mind and may not seem sensible, but you will see different outcomes. If you have clear dreams they will guide your intuition as to your next step. We all can think of experiences we would like in this life, those that we have locked away because we believed they weren't possible. As you unlock those dreams, select the people with whom you share them very carefully; many people will tell you to be sensible and that you shouldn't aim so high.

Life is not about choosing the easiest path; it is about choosing the option that will make you happiest. I know several mothers who have gone back to university to study because that felt right. To go back and study for an extra few years of your life can seem like a long time. However, if your heart knows that is right for you, then make that decision and commit...and commit to feeling good along the way. Some of those decisions will feel good now but will require determination to see them through. With your bigger picture dream, it's easier to practice delayed gratification and persevere.

What are my options?

Your options are limitless, but they will be limited by whatever you think is an option. Some goals will take longer than others, but it's all there for you if you can trust and believe that you can do it. Your perception will be limited mostly by your thinking around the time, money and energy you believe you need to dedicate. These are the three main resources we consider when deciding what we want to do and where we want to go in life. Your success will depend upon the commitment you make to your dream. It will also depend on how willing you are to let go of control. We don't know the way our dream will come into being. By letting go of knowing how, you can free your mind from limitations and be honest about your dream. Instead of contemplating what you believe will fit into your life, decide what you want in your life. Know that somehow the universe will conspire to make sure that things happen to help your dreams come true and that you are supported in whatever decision you want to make.

We live in a technological age where there are no barriers to achieving anything. You have access to people around the world through the Internet. There's no pressure to be bigger or better than anyone else and there are no right or wrong goals. Most important is that we are happy with the goals that we set and that they make our heart sing. Don't dismiss anything because you don't know how it will happen. Be clear about all the different options, and then choose those that feel best for you.

Commitment

Many of us make decisions that we then break. We make New Year's resolutions and keep them for a week or two before slipping back into old habits. Many people wish for things to be different in their lives but aren't committed to creating that change. Our commitment to a decision determines whether or not we will be successful. To fulfill your dreams, you need to follow through on the actions that make the decision come alive even when the initial excitement has passed. If you are content with your lifestyle and don't want to change, be honest and stop wishing for change. Be happy with the choices you make and enjoy life. When you make a decision and don't follow it through, a part of you deep inside knows whether you are committed to it. Not following through with action leaves us feeling that we've failed and it becomes another example of us feeling that we are not "good enough".

When I was a teenager I used to play cricket in a women's team. I loved playing cricket! I decided I wanted to play for the State team. I was about 16 years old and wasn't good enough to make the team…yet. However, I was committed to this decision and wanted it badly. That summer, my boyfriend and I went out training for hours and hours every day. It was one of the best summers of my life – we were outside every day, focused on the end goal and having fun in the moment. We focused on getting our techniques right and improving as far as we could on every aspect of our game. The next time I tried out for the state team I had improved greatly and I made the team. It was such an exciting time for me. If I hadn't been committed to that decision, I know that it would have been another of those things in life that I wished for but that would never have eventuated.

If there are things you truly want in your life, you need to be committed to take inspired action and do whatever it takes. Some of you may only be seeking small changes – if that's the case you still need to be committed to take actions to make those changes. If you are not willing to change your life, then you are not committed to your dream. Your life is important…dreams and goals are not something you give up on. If you really want something, do whatever it takes to stay motivated and focused on your goal.

We are exposed to a huge range of opportunities in our lifetime and sometimes we want to try things before committing fully to them. It's great to try things and be playful with life as long as we have the right approach and mindset. Often times when we "try" something we allow the possibility of failing. This can become an excuse we use; as in "at least I made the effort and gave it a go." Without realizing it, our thinking, feeling and beliefs may have sabotaged our success. We are supposed to play in this earthly playground, have fun and try different things. We are supposed to do so with a mindset that we are enjoying what we choose regardless of the outcome, not using "failure" as a reason to not to do things. Beware of your mindset towards trying new things. Ensure that, if you are "trying" something, your mindset is strong and you know what you want to get out of the experience. Enjoy the experience and allow it to be whatever it needs to be.

Life will change

Once you decide on a path of goal setting and dream building, your life will change. Many people fear change because it's unknown. When you become focused on a goal the decisions you make will differ from those you made in the past, and they will lead to different outcomes. What will change most of all, however, is what's happening inside you. When you commit to living a happy, fulfilling life there is an inherent understanding that life will change. Not everyone around you will feel the same way and some may even resist the change. This can cause doubt to enter your mind. Knowing this means you can prepare for it. Your job is to create a life that makes YOU feel happy and fulfilled. Of course, we want our children to experience a happy, fulfilling life as well, but in the end, we cannot do that for them. You are a role model, and you can give them the best start possible, but you can't make them happy. Imagine if each individual in the world could recognize that happiness is a choice that everyone is entitled to make. Only you can decide how much your dreams are worth and how much you are willing to change to fulfill them.

What if I can't do it?

Your mindset is so important when making a decision. If you think you can't do whatever it is you want, you will create that experience and you won't be able to do it. If you make a consistent and persistent effort, you can do whatever you decide to do. It may take some time, and you may need to learn some new skills and have some setbacks and experiences along the way, but you can do it. It's only your thoughts and beliefs that will stop you from achieving. If you identify a fear that is blocking you it's time to go inside and ask where that fear comes from. You may need to undertake some energy healing work to overcome the fears. There are some amazing light-workers in the world who can help clear energy if you don't know how yourself.

We are the driving force in our own life. When we are working toward our goals we have our ego to contend with along with societal beliefs and expectations. We have our own fears and our thoughts and beliefs that can interrupt our mission. We have old patterns that keep us living in a particular way. You cannot change these unless you are aware of them. But once you are aware, then you start to take responsibility for your power and your destiny.

Chapter Summary

Only by making decisions can we change and move towards our dreams; otherwise we are merely wishing for change. Remember our aim is to feel good, so any decision we make must also feel good and should be guided by our intuition. Our decisions become much clearer if we have a vision – make a vision board and a dream book that include pictures that represent the things you want in life. Use these to inspire you and remind yourself what you are working towards. Even if you don't see the full picture right now it will develop if you work at it.

We all have routines and behavior patterns that bring about the same experiences over and over. One of the easiest ways to create small change is to vary your routine. Any change will do! Cook different meals, talk to different people, move your furniture around or read different books. When you make small changes you become more comfortable with change and it keeps life exciting.

Decision Paralysis is a problem for many people. It can feel easier to not make a decision than to take responsibility for your life. Most of the time people make decisions that are based on fear – it is easier to believe that life happens to us than that we create it. Once we realize that we are creators, we have to take responsibility for everything in our life - that can be daunting for many people.

Deep down in your heart are dreams that you have hidden from the world, even from yourself. Only you can know what you really want out of life. Some things may seem impossible; with others you just can't work out how they will come into your life. Stop worrying about that; focus instead on what you really want – start by developing a very clear vision of it, then your decisions will come more easily. You can be, do or have anything you want; it really is only limited by your own imagination.

There is a difference between dreams and wishes. Many people wish things to be different in their life but are not prepared to change anything to make it happen. If you want change, you will have to commit to it. This may mean putting time, money and energy into whatever it is you want. This commitment must be ongoing and part of that commitment is to feel good whenever you are taking action. When you truly believe in your dream and know it's coming, it's easy to feel good. If you aren't feeling good, there is some doubt. If you are feeling doubt, then you need to work on clearing the doubt and feeling good again. There is no point making decisions and taking actions if you feel doubt.

When you begin working towards your dreams you must be prepared to change for that is the point of it all. If you are not willing to change, that's fine, but admit it and then enjoy the life you have created. If you have doubt and fears about creating change, address these – go and see a healer or an energy worker…do whatever you need to remove the doubt and fear. There is nothing you have to do, other than take responsibility for everything you do.

Questions for self-reflection

1. What decisions have I been putting off in my life?

_____

_____

_____

_____

_____

2. What commitments am I willing to make?

_____

_____

_____

_____

3. What am I prepared to change in my thinking to start making different decisions?

_____

_____

_____

_____

_____

CHAPTER 11

MANAGE YOUR ENERGY

Energy is infinite. It is a medium by which we connect with others and to our source. As we deepen our understanding of energy, we see that it is everything.

I have always been a very high-energy person. I like to do lots of things in my life and I have a real zest and joy about life. When I became a mother, I needed a different sort of energy, particularly when the children were babies. I needed a lot of physical energy just to manage the routines that my babies needed – the sleeping, feeding and making sure they were comfortable, on top of trying to look after myself. As my children began going to school the challenge became mental and emotional.

We are all energy. The way that we can use energy in our lives and the energy that we feel depends very much on our attitude. In this chapter I'm going to take you through some things you can do to improve your energy on a physical, as well as on a mental and emotional level. Energy circulates in your body through a network of energy channels. When we have an intense emotional experience the flow of energy can be disrupted, blocked or even reversed. As we grow more in tune with the energy flow of our bodies we can sense when disruptions occur. We even store energetic memories, many times in a way that's not appropriate for us to function at our peak capacity. When energy is not flowing in its optimum pattern, we see it reflected in our body as physical illness and emotional disharmony.

Our energy needs to recharge like a battery. It does this when we are asleep, and the optimal position for sleeping is to be lying down. If you have ever been trying to sleep on a long plane trip, you know you can feel a difference.

As an energy healer, I see people with all sorts of different aliments - physical, mental and emotional. My children love when I do energy work on them because they can feel a change very quickly. Healing helps our energy realign and flow in the optimum pattern for our health. Healing can help clear thought patterns, fears and phobias, emotional disharmony and physical ailments. It would be lovely to see more Western medical practitioners embrace energetic techniques in their practice.

The DNA influence

There has been much research trying to unlock the codes of our DNA (Deoxyribonucleic Acid). Scientists working with the US military performed one of the experiments that helped my learning. They wanted to test whether the power of our emotions has an effect on our DNA once cells are no longer part of the human body. They took some DNA from a person and, using a specially designed chamber, measured electrically to see if the DNA still responded to the donor's emotions. The DNA donor was taken to a room well away from the DNA sample and was hooked up to a machine that could measure electrical changes. They were then subjected to images that would elicit an emotional response such as happiness, sadness, peace and anger. What they found was that the DNA sample in the other room went through exactly the same electrical peaks and troughs as the person. There was no delay in the peaks and troughs occurring – it was not as though the person was sending a message to their DNA that created the change - it happened at exactly the same time. Similar experiments have been performed over longer distances yielding the same results. The results of this experiment suggest that there is an energy field between living tissue; it appears that our cells and our DNA communicate through this field. It also suggests that our emotions influence our DNA even over a distance. All we need to understand is that our emotional state has a far greater impact than simply on our body.

The Heartmath Institute in the U.S conducted the second experiment that led to my deeper understanding of energy. The aim was to record what happens to the DNA as we experience different emotions. DNA strands are capable of lengthening and shortening. The findings showed that when a person is in a negative emotional state i.e. low vibration, their DNA physically tightens (becomes shorter). When people are angry or sad, they are often very tense; their muscles are tight and they can look shorter. By contrast, DNA physically lengthens when in a positive emotional state such as happiness, joy or love. I have seen remarkable transformations occur in people whose emotions were primarily negative switching to positive emotions. If you would like to understand more about these experiments I recommend watching *The Science of Miracles* by Gregg Braden.

We know our emotional state influences our physical body as we have seen in experiments such as those by Dr. Masuru Emoto's experiments (the water experiments), Vladimir Paponin (the light photons), the US military and the Heartmath Institute. We all affect the world around us. Our emotions affect our DNA. This helps to understand why we must feel good as much as possible. If we are not feeling good most of the time, then our main job is to feel better. If we focus on managing our thoughts and emotions, then we are managing our energy.

What you eat and drink

It would be remiss of me to share all this information and not at least mention that what we put into our body also affects our energy. The food that we eat is supposed to be fuel for our bodies – we need certain nutrients, protein, vitamins etc. However, these days with so much processed food being consumed, our bodies are not getting the fuel that it needs to run at an optimal level. A lot of processed foods leave us still feeling hungry so we start to overeat and put on weight, but we are still not nourished. I was very blessed to grow up with a mother who taught us to eat lots of fresh fruit and vegetables and we didn't have much processed food in our house. I am so grateful for that now and I see the same thing happening with my children.

The foods you eat affect your energetic levels as well as your mental and emotional state. There are a lot of chemicals in food that impact upon your mind and body systems. We must be aware of everything we put into our bodies. Ideally, you want to eat as much food as you can that is as close to what nature intended. That means a lot of raw fruit and vegetables. Meat also contains energy;

it contains the energy of the animal that it came from and the experiences that the animal had. You might like to inform yourself about the farm where the animals were bred and raised, whether they were grass fed and had space to roam.

Whatever we put in our mouth and swallow enters our digestive system. Water is the best thing we can drink, but in most places in the world, water needs to be filtered to be drinkable. So many chemicals are added to our water to make it "safe" to drink. Further investigation has taught me that I don't want those chemicals in my body! We should also limit our tea, coffee and alcohol because of the physical effects they have on the body. All of these things affect our energy and our energetic level. I know people who can't wake up in the morning without having coffee first. If you are in that category, realize that you are craving a stimulant for your body. Our physical body should not need a stimulant to wake us up after we have just had a sleep. However, this is socially acceptable, and many people do enjoy the ritual of tea or coffee first thing in the morning. I'm not dishing out advice as to what's best for you; I only suggest that you do some research of your own and take responsibility for what you put in your body. If you are not feeling vibrant, healthy and energetic, do look at what you are eating and drinking and the way that you choose to fuel your body.

Exercise and you

Exercise is the other area I need to briefly mention. Our bodies are meant to move and be physical. Exercise becomes more difficult the longer we leave it and it can be difficult to get moving again. I saw a little comic strip once and it said, "Another day and I missed the gym … that makes 20 years in a row." I had a chuckle at that because it highlights the sort of patterns that we get into. Before we know it, we haven't exercised for weeks, months and then it becomes years and we look back and wonder what happened. We can make exercising fun – it doesn't have to be slogging it out at a gym. You can get exercise from, swimming, yoga, going for a walk, playing sports or jumping on the trampoline.

If you want to increase your energy, you need to move your body, meaning you need to do some exercise. Find a way that feels fun for you so you can enjoy the experience of exercise. Just going for a walk for half an hour every day and looking up (it helps expand your view of the world) can change the way you feel. Most of us know that when we exercise we end up feeling better. If you have gained a bit of weight, it might take a little while to lose it and feel comfortable again. If your goal is to have a healthy body, start small and take little steps doing some exercise every day.

If we think we have no time to exercise, we will create that experience. Remember this is your life, you decide what it looks like, what a day looks like, what your work looks like – you are your own leader. You can choose how much exercise to do, what you eat and drink and your mindset. Ultimately you have the ability to be a vibrant, energetic, successful person if that is what you want.

Supporting yourself

As we take responsibility for our energy levels (and our life!), we can make self-supportive choices. We all need daily inspiration and motivation to become the people we want to be. I have some big dreams I'd like to fulfill; I know I need to stay focused and energetically strong. I listen to motivational audios, read books and occasionally watch inspirational videos to support me. I am very specific about the books I read and when reading I always attempt to identify the information that feels in alignment with me. I made the decision to join an incredible club that provides me with motivational audios, so I am never short of listening material. This alone has changed my mindset, attitude and increased my awareness of the way I operate in the world. I also meet with like-minded people who support each other. When I am around those people we have fun, we all learn from each other and create a mastermind. A mastermind is a group of people who get together for the same purpose – our purpose is to create the vibration we need to fulfill our dreams. As you define what you want, be aware of people around you – are they supportive of your dreams or content for you to continue living the way you are? When you begin to change, it can become uncomfortable with your friends; you may experience some natural shifts in your friendships.

Your friends are one of your support groups. Yet most of us simply want our friends to buy into our story. If we feel we have been wronged in life we want our friends to say "poor you." It is not supportive to keep us feeling like a victim. It is more supportive to gently help each other take responsibility for what we create and move us back to a place of feeling good. Remember our response to a situation is most important, not the situation itself.

It is also imperative to recognize you have choices. We all have choice, albeit at all different levels. At a mental level, be aware that every word and every thought generates a vibrational message that we send out into the universe. We need to do whatever it takes to think positively, speak positive words and to make sure that our vibration is increasing.

What we eat and drink as well as how we exercise affect us. We choose whether we eat processed food and sugars or whether we eat fresh, healthy options. The sheer recognition that you have a choice is empowering! If you want to make unhealthy choices that's okay as long as you take ownership of your choices.

Our aim is to maintain and increase our vibration; we need to support ourselves to do this. This support is different for each individual, but it is really anything that will help keep you feeling happy (with the exception of drugs and alcohol which mask our true emotions). The more you maintain a positive emotional state, the more you will begin to see what you want to come into your life. It is preferable to achieve sustainable change - long-term change that enables you to create the future you want.

Lighten up!

As adults we become very serious about life; we have bills to pay, children to look after, a house to manage and a host of other things. In developing that seriousness we forget about the lighter fun side of life. It's really important to have fun, to lighten our perspective of the world and enjoy the experiences of life. There is a tendency to derive meaning from everything especially from "bad" situations. Sometimes just being playful is enough to shift our energy allowing us to focus on what we want.

Having fun means that we are in the moment; we forget all the things that we can't do or that we are not doing well. One of my favorite quotes by Ed Foreman is "worry is nothing more than the misuse of your imagination." We worry about a past that we can't change and a future that we are in process of creating. If we are worried, we are more likely to create a negative situation. Worry is one of the biggest time and energy wasters that stops us from enjoying the present moment and focusing on what we want to feel.

Emotional Bank Account

Everyone in the world deserves to feel the love that is needed to reach our potential. At a minimum we need to feel good; to accomplish that we need to spend more time feeling positive emotions than negative emotions. The balance will change from day to day, but the aim is to feel positive most of the time. Your emotional state can be likened to a bank account. The more deposits you make, the higher your vibrational state will be. Deposits can be made through positive words and thoughts, audios, books, energy work, affirmations and any activities that feel good.

We make withdrawals EVERY time we think or speak negatively about others or ourselves and when we make choices that are not in alignment with our highest good. Those small comments we might think or say out loud about our appearance, personality and knowledge etc. all impact upon how we feel. For example, when you drop something and say, "I'm so stupid," you are reinforcing this idea in your brain. Your job is to love you and support you in whatever way you need. This means committing to making more deposits than withdrawals to maintain a positive emotional state.

Energetic Blocks

Energy flows in a specific pattern throughout our physical body. When we have a negative emotional experience, our energy flow can become blocked or flow in the wrong direction. Repeated experiences can create energetic patterns. We need to address these blocks and patterns as we are moving through life as they can keep us from fulfilling our potential and keep us feeling fearful or unworthy.

There are tools we can use to clear energy blocks. The Emotional Freedom Technique (EFT) is very effective; you can learn it quickly and easily. There are hundreds of YouTube videos from which to learn EFT, and there are many practitioners and teachers throughout the world. EFT can help clear emotional blockages, overcome fears, phobias, physical issues and anything else that cause negative emotional states. There are many other forms of energy therapy that can also help to clear blocks. I primarily use EFT, Bio Energetic Synchronization Technique (B.E.S.T) or Simply Healed.

When I first began energy work, I would regularly consult energy healers. They helped me clear old patterns and could help identify some of my energetic blocks and patterns that were holding me back. You are responsible for ensuring that your energy is flowing for your optimum health.

Commit to feeling good

This is one of the best ways to support yourself and raise your vibration. Are you prepared to do whatever it takes to feel good? There are moments when I become angry with my children or I am feeling frustrated, and it's easier to stay in that emotion than to pull myself out of it. I remind myself of my commitment to feel good because I will do whatever it takes to be happy. What it takes varies. Sometimes it will mean playing with my children; it might be cooking my favorite meal, watching an inspiring YouTube video or going outside for a walk. I use the emotional scale as a guide and consistently work on improving my emotion. If you do nothing else but commit to feeling good every day, your life will change. It may not change dramatically at first, but the more you work at it the better you feel.

You influence how you feel through your thoughts, your actions and the clarity of your vision for your life. These are all your choices; no one can choose for you. If you commit to feeling good, you may need to reevaluate some things in your life. What you eat, what you drink, who you socialize with, what you read, who you listen to – all of those external things can impact on whether or not you feel good.

Only you can know your vision for your life. The more you take responsibility for this and take steps toward creating it, the more empowered you will feel. You have the power to change at any point in time. You do not have to be a slave to any old emotional hang-ups or any other patterns you carried in your life. You do not have to be afraid that you can't succeed or that you are not good enough. Anyone, including you, can make the changes they want. By committing to feeling good you will take great strides toward creating that change in your life now.

Overcoming feeling tired

As mothers we are physically challenged by all we have to do as well as being responsible for our children's wellbeing. I have very high energy levels so I manage to do most of the things I want. At times, I get very tired; that is when I know I must take better care of my own needs. All the tools and ideas in this book can help shift your energy, but the most important thing is to change your mindset about being tired. We get into a mode of being tired, often when our children are babies and we lose many a night's sleep. We then adopt poor habits because we feel tired. We might stop exercising, watch television every night or drive everywhere instead of walking. Visualize yourself as an energetic vibrant person and commit to feeling good. The more you do this, the more you will find your energy levels rise.

Your energy can be determined for the day from the moment you wake up and get out of bed. If you wake up and crawl out of bed feeling lethargic and uninspired, your energy levels will immediately be low. If you jump out of bed, read an inspirational quote, look in the mirror and say, "I love you," you will set yourself up for a better day energetically. We need to nurture ourselves, beginning from the moment we wake up. Try different routines when you wake until you find what works for you. There's a few different things I'll do – I might exercise early, listen to motivational audios, listen to music, smile at myself in the mirror, read an inspiring book or walk the dog – whatever feels right for that day.

Natural peaks and troughs

We all experience energetic peaks, troughs, situations that challenge us and other experiences that lift our spirit. This is a normal human experience. Most important is how long we decide to stay in the trough. This is highly influenced by the way that we think about situations and our underlying beliefs. When we can look at situations in a positive light, no matter how bad they might seem we can maintain a more positive emotional state.

When we have more trust in what's happening and understand that our emotions help to create our experiences, we gain a glimpse of the importance of our emotional state. It becomes obvious that we need to choose to move out of negative or low vibrational states as quickly as possible. The longer we remain confused about what we want to do with our life, the further away our goals and dreams are. The longer we stay angry, hurt, guilty or sad, the more we tell the universe that we don't believe we are worthy of living the life of our dreams. By contrast, the longer we stay happy, the more we create happy experiences. It is as if we have two balls of energy – one negative and one positive. You want the positive ball to be bigger than the negative. The more you stay in a positive energetic space, the more peace you will experience.

We will still experience times of distress, but we stay in them for shorter time periods – instead of days they will be hours, instead of hours they will be minutes. You can raise your natural vibrational state over time by improving your energy, thoughts and feelings. The main reason we experience those peaks and troughs is that we have moved out of trust and we don't believe that our vision can come to fruition.

Trust in the process

One of the most valuable lessons I've learnt is to trust everything that happens in my life. I know that we can make good of every situation even in the worst of circumstances. Once you have chosen your life vision, you must hold that vision and know without doubt that it is coming into your life. When I lost my job unexpectedly one day, I couldn't believe that was possibly for my highest good. I could only see that I didn't have an income. I have, however, found that the job loss forced me to clear a lot of emotional baggage that I had been carrying around about friendship, security and what I really wanted to do. It propelled me very quickly to move on with what I really wanted in my life. In the end it was such a blessing because it's opened up new opportunities that I might otherwise not have taken.

Every time you are in doubt, you send a conflicting message to the universe. Worry generally comes from your imagination rather than from what is really happening in your life. The natural peaks and troughs of your energy or your emotional state change many times throughout a day, but if you can trust in yourself to overcome the lows and know that life is a journey, you will stay in the peaks longer. Trust is a choice like everything else. It can be extremely difficult to maintain your sense of trust and love when very difficult circumstances occur, but to do so will help you emotionally and mentally.

Chapter Summary

Energy literally flows in a regular pattern through your body. The choices you make every day affect this flow, which in turn can affect how you feel. Experiments have shown that our DNA experiences peaks and troughs according to our emotional state, and this experience continues whether or not it is still physically connected to our body. DNA is also physically influenced in its length by our emotions.

With the state of the food industry in our world relatively few people are nutritionally sustained so they can perform at their optimum level. What you eat and drink affects your energy levels. Notice next time you eat take away food – does it make you feel energized or energy-depleted? You are responsible for what you put in your body; do the research and become more aware of the effect it really has on your energy. Exercise is essential for the human body. We are not supposed to sit at a desk for 10 hours a day! We need to move our body, keep it fit and flexible. It makes an enormous difference to our energy levels if we are carrying extra weight or are physically unfit.

To stay motivated, inspired and focused on our dreams we need to support ourselves…every day. This can be in any form that you find supportive. On a mental and emotional level it will help to listen to motivational audios, read books and attend live functions with supportive people. On a physical level the choices you make about food, drink, exercise and the way you think will all contribute to your energetic health.

Life is supposed to be fun. We are supposed to laugh every day and enjoy ourselves. If you have become overly serious about life, worry a lot and have forgotten how to laugh, find some things to help you lighten up. Remember you create your experiences from your thinking and emotional states!

Imagine your energy as an emotional bank account. The more positive words, thoughts and actions you deposit, the better you will feel. Conversely, the more negative ideas you think about and low vibrational emotions you feel, the worse you will feel. The negative always acts like a withdrawal from your emotional bank account. If you are feeling negative, use it to clarify what you do want in life and work your way back up the emotional scale.

As we have all experienced situations that we reacted to negatively at an emotional level, we all have energetic blocks in our system. It is possible to clear these blocks many energetic healing techniques. The techniques I favor are Emotional Freedom Technique (EFT), Bio Energetic Synchronization Technique (B.E.S.T) and Simply Healed.

Your energetic health is your responsibility. You can mange it through all of the different choices you make, from when you wake up through to how you sleep at night. At any moment of a day you can commit to feeling good. It's not always easy, but it is always worth it! This means you notice how you are thinking and feeling and if you are in a low vibrational state you do whatever it takes to feel better. You have energetic patterns and habits, so it may take time to change but the more you work on it the easier it becomes. Your commitment to you and your health is totally your choice.

We will all experience natural peaks and troughs in our energy levels. We are not used to listening to what our body needs and providing it. For example, many times when we are hungry our body is actually slightly dehydrated and craving water. We can choose how long we stay in a trough for and the more you practice energy techniques the faster you will be able to shift back towards a peak. The more you can trust what is happening in your life the more empowered you will feel.

Questions for reflection

1. What am I doing to support myself energetically?

_____

_____

_____

_____

_____

2. What do I commit to thinking and doing to feel good?

_____

_____

_____

_____

_____

3. What patterns do I notice about my energetic peaks and troughs?

_____

_____

_____

_____

_____

CHAPTER 12

GETTING INTO ACTION

Action without vision creates a busy life. Action with vision creates a successful life. It is time to engage in meaningful actions and enjoy every step of the way

There are two types of action

1. Internal actions: these encompass our thoughts, feelings, visions and attitude. For example, when writing a book the internal actions include creating a vision, considering what stories to inject, feeling good about the writing process, etc.
2. External actions: these include the physical actions we take. For example, writing the book, cover design, marketing, etc.

Many of us lead busy lives and are constantly in action. If your thinking, feelings and attitude are not aligned with your dream and your vision, your actions won't be focused and you may not be moving toward what you want. By contrast, if your vision is clear and aligned with your thoughts and actions, you can make change in your life very quickly. Most of us tend to focus on the external actions – on what we need to do next to make things happen – this is because we try to control so much in our lives. We believe that, in order to succeed, we must be in constant action.

Slowing down and making sure that your thoughts and feelings are in alignment with what you want is invaluable. You will move toward your dreams far more quickly when you get that part right. This is not to say you shouldn't take action until your thoughts are perfect…rather work on defining the dream first and feeling good about it. When an opportunity comes you will then be poised to take advantage of it. I had been thinking about writing a book for many years. But I didn't feel confident I could write a valuable book! Instead I clarified my dreams in life and reached a point where I was feeling great most of the time. I wasn't even thinking about writing a book when an opportunity presented itself. I knew immediately this was the perfect time to take action and write. If I had tried to push the external action of writing earlier, it probably would have been quite laborious rather than proving an enjoyable process.

There is nothing that you *have* to do

You don't have to make any changes if you don't want; it is an entirely personal decision. If you tune in to your intuition and get a very clear "No, this is not the time to take this step," listen to it. Likewise, if your intuition says, "Yes, get moving," then follow that feeling. If your decision is to do nothing right now, then just start by feeling good or feeling better in your life. If your decision is to take action and move toward a career change, lose weight, establish a business or anything else, just commit to that decision.

Creating your vision

I've made it clear throughout the book that it's important we have a clear vision of what we want in life in order to take the right action steps. It might sound simple but we cannot create the life we want if we don't know what it looks like. One of my favorite activities to do with my children is to go dream building. We have a look at the things that we would like and enjoy the process. We will go and sit in the cars, walk through the houses or try on the clothes we would like. We experience these things so that we know the feeling of it, but we do so with the understanding that ultimately we just want to feel good. Life is not about the "stuff" that we want…it's always about the feelings.

Create a dream board or a dream book or both! Use pictures, including pictures of people who represent the feelings that you want. If you want to be a happier, more joyful mother, include photographs that inspire you to feel that way. If you want a certain type of car, put a photo of that car on your vision board. Don't judge what you want – just know that you would like the experience of it in this lifetime. When it comes to making a decision about "now what," include your children in the vision without limiting your possibilities. Make sure that you are not creating a vision so as to be "realistic" about what you think is possible. Make sure that your vision makes your heart sing and that it is YOUR vision. As mothers we are so used to looking after everyone else's needs and wants that we forget our own. When you create a vision board it is entirely about what you want in your life, not what anyone else wants.

As you develop your vision, remember to focus on the feeling of what you want, not on the feeling that something is missing from your life. If we have the feeling of something missing when we look at our dream boards, we are creating the experience of not having what we want. This is supposed to be a fun activity; realize that as you grow your vision board will grow with you. My own vision board has changed dramatically over the past year or two as I decided more about what I want and have become more focused on my direction. When I first began, there were some things on my vision board that felt so unrealistic and out of reach that it felt bad when I looked at them, so I needed to put pictures of things that felt a bit more in alignment. As I've grown to understand that we can create anything, I have been able to expand my vision to include things I really want. My children all have their own vision boards that they put pictures on as well. We talk about want we want both as a family and as individuals. When we put photos on the vision board that represent what we want as a family, we effectively create a mastermind so we become a really powerful force.

Taking baby steps

When you do move into the external action, you don't have to create great change very quickly, although you can if you want and if that feels right. Most people prefer gradual change so they are comfortable enough to go through the process expanding their vision along the way. As we have a need for controlling our life, we like to see the entire journey to reaching our goal. If we can let go of needing that, the universe can support us in ways that surprise us and ways that we couldn't have imagined.

All we need to know is that next step. When I look back on my corporate days, we needed to produce marketing plans and strategic plans for the following three years. Yet, we typically found that, once we had taken the first step, everything changed, making the rest of the plan obsolete. The same happens to our life. We can take one step, and because the outcome of that step, things change along with everything we thought we knew.

My eldest daughter had an assistant math teacher in her class one day. She had not understood the work she was supposed to do during that lesson. When the assistant teacher came over to her, he told her to get on with it and to stop procrastinating. She tried to explain that she didn't understand it and needed some help, to which he responded that she was treading water and not getting anywhere. My daughter, being my daughter, turned to this teacher and said, "But sir, some people stay alive treading water." She was absolutely right. People do stay alive by treading water; we can all stay alive and continue to do all the things that we have always done. But if you want to swim and move forward, you need to take some action somewhere – you need to move your arms and legs and start taking swimming strokes ... the same way we take guided action.

I have talked about intuition in this book. Guided action is just that, and it is making sure that the steps you take feel good to you and feel like the next logical step. When you rely on your emotions for guidance, you will become very powerful. We are used to taking guided actions in the care of our children. We are less well versed in taking actions that will change our lives in ways that will move us closer to fulfilling our dreams. When you listen to your intuition, let go of it needing to be anything or to make logical sense to your mind. Sometimes I have been guided to get in contact with someone without knowing why at that time. Inevitably I find that it was perfect timing for some reason or another to make contact.

As you make changes, focus on your dreams and move toward what you want, you are likely to have to give up something to make that change. It can be as simple as giving up negative thinking or beliefs that you have held. Following your dreams may mean giving up friends who aren't supportive of the changes you are trying to make. It may mean giving up some time with your children or with your partner, but when you look at what you might need to give up, do so with the focused intention that you are moving toward what you want. Instead of considering it as giving up something, think of it as taking actions that support your dreams.

We all have some habits and things we do that aren't supportive of us moving forward. Now is the time we need to focus on feeling good and to move into trust that we are moving toward what we want. So try to make sure that all of your actions are guided by your *intuition*, not by what you *think* you should be doing, and above all, make sure you feel good.

Stepping out of your comfort zone

When you decide to make changes in your life, you will have to move out of your comfort zone. When my children began school, my comfort zone needed to stretch to move into a new routine. My eldest daughter, Rhian, began school while we lived in Spain. Pupils were taught in the local language, Catalan. That was confronting and took me far out of my comfort zone, but we both found our way through it quickly. Rhian learnt the language within a few months, and I learned to converse well enough with the teachers and found some friends who spoke English whom could help me with translation at times. It wasn't easy, but I know that induced incredible growth for both of us.

Begin to notice areas in which you may be too comfortable, where your lifestyle doesn't fit in with your vision for the future. Choose one such area that you want to change, but also one that does not feel like will be overwhelming.

A simple process might include:

Step 1: Get clear about where you are now. For example:

    a) If you want to lose weight you need to know how much y you weigh

    b) If you want to find a job, know what skills you enjoy using most

Step 2: Get a clear vision of what you want. In the first example you might choose a target weight, a health goal or gather pictures of how you would like to look. In the second example, know all the things you want in a job; everything from the hours you work, the skills you use, the people you work with, location, etc.

Step 3: Take the first step within 48 hours of making a decision. The action can be whatever your intuition tells you should be your next step. If you do not take action within that period of time, your psyche will put it down to another thing you would have liked to do but I didn't get round to. Whereas when you take action within 48 hours you are committing to make the changes in your life that you really want.

Activity cycles

When Rhian was very young, I used to take her to the wave pool. Every 15 minutes a siren would blast and there would be manmade waves for 15 minutes. When the waves died down the pool would be calm like a normal swimming pool. Fifteen minutes later the cycle would repeat. Everyone would rush into the water because they wanted to play with the waves, but when it was turned off, a lot of people would get out of the water – it certainly wasn't as fun as playing in the waves.

Ideally we want to take action in cycles, much like those waves. It becomes more exciting when we think of it in terms of a cycle because we know at the end of that cycle there will be some kind of result. It also allows us to monitor the progress of the action because we can look at our actions in terms of a cycle. Whatever it is you have determined to be a cycle, you have a period of activity that you can look back on and decide whether to continue or to change the activity. The main thing is that we take some action and we take note of what happens. Our job is to become more conscious of the way we are living, more conscious of our thoughts, our actions, and the outcomes. As you move into action, set yourself an activity cycle. If you want to lose weight you might set a 30-day activity cycle and then measure progress. If you want a new job you might spend a certain number of hours networking, applying for jobs, etc. Regardless of whether the action you need to take is internal or external, you can start taking that action now.

Monitoring progress

It is important that we have some way of knowing we are creating change. If we commit to feeling good all the time, how will we know that we have actually shifted and feel better than we did before? When I first began to make internal shifts, especially around feeling happier, I was unable to recognize how far I had come. This was because situations that had felt really bad no longer felt that way. But unless I could recall my starting point I didn't necessarily see the shift.

Most importantly, create a measuring system that supports you and works for you. That is, find a way to keep track of the target activity and note your successes daily. This helps you to know exactly what you have achieved and also to stay focused on the positive change. One measuring system I use is my diary system by which I reflect on my achievements and successes every day. I also use other forms of measurement to break my bigger goals into steps such as charts that I can mark when I have completed something. There are innumerable ways you can monitor your winning attitude each day. When you decide upon your actions, make sure they are "winnable" i.e. they are achievable. Then, when you reflect back on your day you begin to feel successful which, in turn, creates a strong mental attitude that gives you confidence. You choose what success means to you and what rules you will play by in your life.

I used to set big goals and, when I failed to reach them the first time, I was left feeling like my efforts had not worked. I didn't realize that I needed to divide the activity into a daily, weekly or monthly cycle in order to create a feeling of success. The way I had defined success meant I didn't see how my actions fitted into a bigger picture, and I had no accurate way of measuring my achievements. This did not support me at all; it served only to make me feel small. It stopped me from sharing more of myself with the world and more of the information I knew. Whatever method you choose to measure your success, make sure it is easy for you to win and that it supports you in building your confidence.

Your support network

If you want support from friends and you don't have it, you will need to find some new friends or people who will support you. It doesn't mean you have to give up your old friends, but you may find that, as your vibration increases and you feel happier, your old friends will naturally disappear or you spend less time with them. It's also imperative that you spend some time every week with your support network. This will help to keep you inspired, raise your vibration and stay on track. They can become your accountability partners – you can tell them what actions you want to take and they can check that you did take those actions.

It is essential your support network gives you a feeling of being in a safe space. If you are going to share your dreams, you want to know that you are being supported and not judged. You want to feel absolute trust in your group, and you will also want to support the others creating their dreams. You don't have to share the specifics of your dreams with the group; they can be supportive just by cheering you along the journey and celebrating your successes without knowing all of the details. You will find it refreshing and it will open up your mind and your heart in ways you might not have expected. It is wonderful to know that you can call someone who you know will offer support when you are having a bad day. You develop a closer relationship with these people because you are sharing a very personal journey.

There are many ways you can form a support group. You can join an established group or create one yourself. You might join a club, a coaching group, organize a meet-up group, create a Facebook group or Google hangout group. With current technologies, you don't even have to live in the same geographical area. However, there is much power in physically being together regularly as you implement your life changes.

All things must come from love

Whatever you want to create in your life, it will become more powerful if you do so from a place of love. If you want to become an artist and express yourself, doing so from a place of love will reveal a different energy in your creations. If you want to help other people in some way, doing so from a place of love rather than from a place of "I need to make money", will change the energy of your actions. Inevitably you will find that actions taken from love makes the money flow in unexpected ways.

Ultimately we want love in our life, regardless of whether it is love for self, love for others or love from others. Love is the key to a better world. It is the vibration that can help stop wars, heal old wounds and old hurts. It can repair marriages and relationships with children. It can return us to a place where we feel whole again. This may sound a little airy-fairy to some, but the more you practice love, the more love you will bring into your life. So when you decide on your next step, make sure it originates in a place of love for yourself, for your family and for the vision of what you want in your life

Feeling like a whole person

As a mother you will naturally consider all of your decisions in the context of your family and children, but you also need make sure they are what you want as an individual. When I imagine my vision it always includes my children. They are an integral part of my life, but I also have another side to me that I want to share with the world. I have discovered that the more I find my bliss, the more others around me do so as well. The more I get in touch with my creative side, the more my children have permission to get in touch with theirs and the more inspired they are to pursue the things they want.

While we need to consider others, we also must cater to our needs and follow our dreams and desires. If your bliss is motherhood, then be a mother with your whole heart, without judging whether you should be working or doing more in the community. Enjoy what you are doing and feel good about living your life vision, because everyone, including stay-at-home mothers, needs to have a vision of the way they want life to look. If your bliss includes working, then do that with your whole heart. Find a job you are passionate about or start a business and make sure you work the hours that suit you. At times, this seems challenging, but it is really only limited by your beliefs, your thoughts, and your perception of what is possible. If you want to be working full-time then enjoy every moment while you are there and be fully present and enjoy your children when you are with them. The more you nurture yourself as the whole person you are, the more you can fulfil your needs and grant others permission to do the same.

Education versus entertainment

Learning is a lifetime pursuit; it's not something confined to school that then stops as we grow older and leave school. We are free to focus our learning on the things that interest us most. When you became a mother, you might have stopped the process of deliberate learning and focused on learning about being a mother. If you find yourself in a position now where you need or want to learn new skills or acquire new knowledge, it can feel overwhelming. Keep in mind your life vision and break any study into achievable steps. I recently studied for a new certification; ticking off each accomplished module as I went was so much fun.

Every day, I try to do at least one thing that contributes to my learning. I might simply read an article or a book, listen to an audio recording or talk with people in my support network. When you focus on learning, you grow and develop in unexpected ways. If it doesn't interest you to learn, that's okay too. Notice, though, if you choose to spend a lot of time being entertained – that is often a sign that we have no dreams. Entertainment comes in many forms nowadays; it includes everything from television, YouTube videos, phone apps and magazines. If you live a blissful life and all you want is to be entertained, then enjoy it. Remember that success is whatever you define it to be. In general however, although successful and empowered people will enjoy entertainment, they don't spend most of their time being entertained, especially not by the media. They spend most of their time having fun, being educated and inspired, being with supportive, like-minded people, and they are open to new opportunities that come their way.

Distractions on the path

For many years, my focus was entirely on my children, which is what I always wanted. More recently, I have allowed myself to be quite distracted from my dreams by looking after the children, cleaning my house, participating in a lot of voluntary work, hanging out with friends, etc. This was because I hadn't defined my dreams – I was simply "getting through" life. I completed some amazing projects during that time. But once I defined my dreams, I could see how much I had allowed those distractions to take me off the path my heart wanted to follow. I hid behind the distractions and used them as excuses. Using my diary system has helped me to focus my attention, thoughts and actions on what I truly want. As I look back, I realize that I used all those distractions because I was fearful of moving forward. I had lost confidence in myself and I wasn't sure I could achieve what I really wanted. I was not confident of being able to make the changes and still be the mother I wanted to be for my children. The dream could always stay on the sideline waiting until the day I had the courage to begin a new journey. Now I choose to focus my attention, stop those distractions and focus on an activity, internal and external, that supports my dream. Do look at your own life: are there things you allow to distract you? And are there changes you need make to overcome those hurdles?

Stay in alignment in thought and action

Our creations will be more powerful if we allow ourselves to experience the feelings we imagine will exist as we accomplish our goals, even before we reach those goals. If we have a vision for a particular job, we need to feel the feelings we expect to have when we get that job. If we expect to feel bliss, happiness and gratitude when we are working, we need to bring those feelings to the present moment. This is where you can use tools like the Heartmath Quick Coherence technique (see Chapter 5) to bring about that feeling. Your thinking is key to your decision to move forward. You make decisions about your future every day without even realizing it. When you are in alignment with your dreams, then you will be focused on priorities to work toward those dreams. Stop thinking about what is possible and think about what you really want. Make your decisions based upon what you really want from your heart, not what you think is realistic or achievable. Dream bigger and have fun with it!

If you have not yet been able to clarify your dreams and you have to go out to work for the time being, see work as a temporary stopgap. It will give you relief from financial pressure as you define your dream and your next steps. If you choose to dream only about what is possible right now, you will continue to limit yourself. The alignment comes when you stay in a positive mindset and believe that your dreams are all becoming a reality. If you keep on doubting or you worry about the future, you are sending mixed messages out into the universe. As a consequence, your energy will feel scattered. When in alignment, you will feel more driven than you have in the past, and your actions will move you closer to your dreams

Double-check those beliefs

Beliefs are one of the major blocks that keep us stuck and limit our possibilities. Remember that a belief is simply a thought that you think over and over and over, like a never-ending record playing in your head. You have been carrying the energy of the thought, thereby repeatedly experiencing events supporting that thought, allowing it to evolve into a belief. We all have beliefs that aren't serving us and that we therefore need to shift. Of course, we can't change a belief unless we are aware that we have it. We need constantly to monitor and check in with ourselves around our belief patterns. If a particular experience keeps recurring that you don't want in life, there is definitely a belief that is not serving you.

Energetically, you can address the energy of your beliefs very quickly using EFT (Emotional Freedom Technique), TFT (Thought Field Therapy) or several other energetic techniques. You can also change your beliefs by focusing on new and better thoughts for 21-30 days, the time it takes to change the neural pathway. Anytime you think something is impossible, that your dream is too big or you can't fulfill it, there is a belief you need to change. The more you manage to clear old limiting beliefs and replace them with new empowering ones, the easier it will be for you to create the life of your dreams.

Chapter Summary

Actions take place at two levels–internally or externally. Internal actions involve our thoughts, feelings, dreams and attitudes. External actions include any physical actions such as making telephone calls, writing applications or applying for loans. Internal actions are by far the most important because they influence the outcome of the external actions.

No one has to make any change to his or her life. But if you want more out of life and have some dreams, now is a great time to begin taking action even, or should I say especially, internal action.

Spend time defining your vision and know it will grow as you see more possibilities. Create a vision board and a dream book and fill them with pictures that reflect what you want. You can include anything that you want in these – any picture that captures the feelings of the "stuff" you would like to experience. Dream big and as you expand your vision, dream bigger!

You don't have to make big changes or jump into an entirely new life, unless that is what you want. Changes can be made on a smaller level such as changing your routine. Break your actions into smaller cycles. This way you can measure your progress and your tasks will not seem as overwhelming. Your activity cycle can be for a period of time such as a week or month, or doing something a specific number of times such as sending twenty resumes.

To create change and follow the journey to fulfill your dreams you will need to move out of your comfort zone. It has been well established for many years. For many mothers, it shrank upon becoming a mother as we had a new life to consider. You can choose to take giant leaps or small steps to moving out of the zone.

In all things you have choice. Feeling successful is especially important along the journey, as this will create more successful situations. The easiest way to feel successful is to create a measuring system where you always win. This means each small task, even at a daily level, counts as a success. If you're applying for jobs you might set yourself a task to send off two resumes a day. At the end of the day if you have done this, you can note it as a success; more importantly, it will feel like success.

We all need a support network, people that we can count on who will cheer us on and help us move forward when we're feeling low. Be mindful of who you share your dreams with as some people are not afraid to tell you they think you can't achieve something. Ideally your support network helps to create a safe space for everyone to share – you don't need to share the specifics but it's fun to share your wins. You can create your own network or join an already established group.

When your thoughts and actions come from a place of love you will be supported in amazing ways. When your dreams come from a place of love for you and your family, you will be more motivated to take those internal and external actions. Love is the most powerful force in the universe. Whatever you do from love will feel better on every level of your being.

As mothers we are used to considering our children and families in all of our decisions. When defining your dream, make sure it is what you really want, regardless of whether you see how it fits in with your family life. If it is in conflict with your family and makes you feel bad, then perhaps it is not what you really want. I am talking about creating a vision that feels in full alignment with all you have to consider, but also a vision that satisfies you at a heart level.

Notice how you spend you time. We all have more to learn, but many people prefer to be entertained than to be educated. Modern society has created an accepted entertainment system through magazines, TV, the Internet and other media. The most successful people in the world do not partake in much media entertainment; they understand that there are more productive and enjoyable ways to be fulfilled. One of the most widespread distractions in our society is through the media. At every point you choose how you spend your time. We use distractions because we are scared of failure or success, we're bored or feel deeply unhappy with our life. It is easier to remain busy and distracted feeling we don't have time for anything else, than to admit we have some dreams that aren't being fulfilled.

Every thought and every action counts! We must, as much as possible, stay in alignment with what we want on a bigger level. The best way is to feel the feelings now that you think you will have when you achieve your dreams. This will bring your dreams closer in leaps and bounds.

We all have beliefs that don't serve us. We need to use whatever techniques we can to clear out the energy associated with these beliefs and change them. The most effective techniques are Emotional Freedom Technique (EFT) and Thought Field Therapy (TFT) – they are simple to learn and easy to learn. Along your journey beliefs will challenge you – just continue to deal with them one-by-one as they show up.

Questions for self-reflection

1. What is my vision for my life in 1 year, 5 years, 10 years?

_____

_____

_____

_____

_____

2. How will I support myself mentally, physically, emotionally?

_____

_____

_____

_____

3. How much is my dream worth to me?

_____

_____

_____

_____

_____

A personal note

I know you can make the changes you want in your life. You can be, do, or have anything you like. In order to understand and use everything in this book, you will need to read it more than once. If you answer the questions at the end of each chapter, they will give good ideas of changes you can begin to make.

Make sure that you love you throughout your journey. There is no other you in the world, no one else with your unique traits and with your abilities. You bring something special and unique to the world, and you deserve to live an inspired life. Start by feeling good every day. Life is meant to be fun, and we are meant to enjoy ourselves. We are meant to be around people who make us laugh, inspire us and make us feel good.

I wish you love as you continue on this beautiful journey that is life. Love your children like nothing else on earth, love yourself in the same way and know you have what it takes to create whatever you want in your life.

FURTHER RESOURCES

These are some resources I have found helpful on my journey. You may find them helpful too.

Books
Ask and it is Given, Esther and Jerry Hicks, 1401904599
The Hidden Messages in Water, Dr Masaru Emoto, 0743289803
The Magic of Believing, Claude M Bristol, 0671745212
The Magic of Thinking Big, David J Schwartz, 0671646788
The Power of Now, Ekhart Tolle, 1577314808

Videos
The Science of Miracles, Gregg Braden
The Secret, Rhonda Byrne

Websites
The Heartmath Institute, www.heartmath.org

ABOUT THE AUTHOR

Margit Cruice is an author, life coach, energy healer and motivational speaker. She works with clients from around to world to transform their lives. She is passionate about living with confidence, clarity and love. She sees LOVE as the basis for life, for achieving your goals and dreams and to be the person you want to be.

In the past she has successfully developed and facilitated courses for mothers finding work/life balance, for children to increase confidence and self-esteem and for women to find their passion.

A Life Coach for 8 years, Margit works on a deep inner level, creating sustainable change. As an Energy Healer she is prepared to work on anything! She believes everyone can have the life of their dreams if they are prepared to make some changes.

With three children all now at school, she has successfully become the mother she always wanted to be and is following her personal path to create the life of her dreams. Margit lives in Noosa, Queensland, Australia.

To contact Margit about her coaching or speaking services visit:
www.margitcruice.com
www.howtoloveLOVEme.com

www.ingramcontent.com/pod-product-compliance
Lightning Source LLC
Chambersburg PA
CBHW061310110426
42742CB00012BA/2133